Teaching in the Land of Kimchi

Discovering South Korea as a Working Ground

by

Melissa Christine Karpinski

PITTSBURGH, PENNSYLVANIA 15222

The contents of this work including, but not limited to, the accuracy of events, people, and places depicted; opinions expressed; permission to use previously published materials included; and any advice given or actions advocated are solely the responsibility of the author, who assumes all liability for said work and indemnifies the publisher against any claims stemming from publication of the work.

All Rights Reserved
Copyright © 2010 by Melissa Christine Karpinski
No part of this book may be reproduced or transmitted in any form or by any means, electronic or mechanical, including photocopying, recording, or by any information storage and retrieval system without permission in writing from the author.

ISBN: 978-1-4349-9798-2
eISBN: 978-1-4349-4148-0
Printed in the United States of America

First Printing

For more information or to order additional books,
please contact:
RoseDog Books
701 Smithfield Street
Pittsburgh, Pennsylvania 15222
U.S.A.
1-800-834-1803
www.rosedogbookstore.com

Acknowledgments

After a long, hellish childhood filled with confusing, emotional, and manipulative adult figures, a few good people and amazing mentors managed to squeeze out of the suffocating bunch and literally save me. The following are the ones who saved me in the latest chapter of my life. They are to whom I dedicate this book.

To my family. Even though they don't understand my actions, they care a great deal.

To Dr. To-Kyu Lee, who motivated me to pursue this book idea especially after I saw how hard he worked to write and edit his own books on veterinary medicine. He is the best veterinarian my pets have ever had. Thank you for making a difference in the life of the precious animals in Korea.

To Ian, who has always seen accomplishment in me and who has loved me unconditionally. He truly and sincerely understands. Thank you for helping me exactly when you knew I needed it, no questions asked.

To Kim Duk June, Michelle, and their sons Danny and Gabriel. They have made my most difficult times in Korea smoother and happier. I value your generosity and kindness, and I fear I can never repay you at the same level.

To KARA (Korea Animal Rights Advocates), for giving me, Gus, and Reese the privilege of participating in events revolving around the issue that is an enormous part of my life: animal welfare and rights. To Yuni and Mr. Bk Zang (and Lassie, Ahjung, Sundori, and Momo); don't stop the anti-dog meat push. Your constant dedication to the neglected animals of Korea is recognized and appreciated by many, especially the animals. Keep up the excellent work!

To the Partida family; Donna, Rocky, Amalia, Julisa, and Mrs. Lewis (Donna's mom), for treating me like one of their own. I'll never forget your hospitality.

To Tom Piper, for recognizing my determination.

Contents

Introduction vii

Chapter 1:
A New Beginning 1
    How and why I chose Korea as a working ground
    Is Korea for you?

Chapter 2:
Know Before You Go: Understanding the Stats and Facts 6
    The E2 Teaching Visa
    How do I get a visa to teach?

Chapter 3:
A Long Way From Home:
Your New Environment and the Culture Around You 10
    An anxious start
    Understanding collectivism in Korea
    The do's and don'ts of housing

Chapter 4:
Getting the Job You Want 16
    Choices, choices; public school, university, or hagwon
    What qualifications do you need?
    The advantage and disadvantage of using a job recruiter

Chapter 5:
Surviving Korean Culture 23
    Perceptions of the other
    Classroom culture What kind of behavior to expect
    The Westerner's perspective of his job
    The impact of support on the ability to adjust

Chapter 6:
The Conundrum of Communication 39
    Communicating with Korean co-workers
    Lost in translation
    Korean vs. Western values
    Coping with your job

Chapter 7:
Business as Usual 58
    The business side of the Korean English school
    Corruption
    English teaching contracts; what you need to know
    Example of the first teaching contract
    Example of the second teaching contract

Chapter 8:
Conversations 76
    Howard from Australia
    Doug from the United States
    Nate from Canada
    Rob from the United States
    Reflections

Chapter 9:
Important Information to Refer to Once You Arrive in Korea 107
    Basic information
    Getting your Korean driver's license
    Opening a bank account
    Questioning yourself: Is it the right decision?

Bibliography 112

Introduction

South Korea is one unbelievable country. In less than sixty years, it has grown into a strong, industrial superpower, with exports rising every year and its products becoming more superior. From LCD displays and electronics, to automobiles and semiconductors, Korean products are becoming recognizable around the world. Export partners include China, Japan, Hong Kong, and the United States, but it doesn't stop there.

Korea is also a story of survival. Its people have lived through war, Japanese occupation, and dictatorship. Amazingly, it is possible to find many elderly Koreans who have experienced all of these events in their adult lifetimes. Since its division at the 38th parallel in 1945, South Korea has seen fast-paced development in culture, entertainment, economy, business, and education. The country has blossomed from one of Asia's poorest to one of its richest.

The people of South Korea are mainly ethnically Korean, however, over the years there has been an influx of foreigners coming to Korea to work. Many of them now consider Korea their home. Korea is generally a homogenous society, but it is changing at a fast pace. I have met numerous children with mixed parents. Some have Japanese or Vietnamese mothers and fathers. There is a constant flow of people from the Philippines, India, Russia, and some other Southeast Asian countries, who are looking for work in prosperous South Korea and hoping to have a better way of life for their families.

South Korea is certainly no back woods country, and it has given me much pleasure and pain to experience it for myself as an expatriate and a teacher. Even through my many bouts of culture-shock, I have learned to appreciate the mix of the traditional with the new, and after spending a few years teaching English to its people, I have found that, actually, it has educated me.

This book has been written with the potential Western expatriate in mind. However, not just the expatriate, but the traveler, teacher, adventurer, businessperson, university graduate, and anyone interested in exploring South Korea as a working ground. Although it focuses on Westerners finding an English teaching job and surviving culturally and professionally in the country, it provides helpful information on what steps to take when seeking out work, how to live comfortably, and what to expect when communicating with Korean people and co-workers. It also details what to watch out for when choosing a job. With South Korea's increasingly developing English education program, it is in constant need of Western English teachers. The need now is in the thousands (approximately eight thousand), and there never seems to be enough applicants.

With the information in this book, I hope to encourage more Westerners to consider Korea as a legitimate place to work, as well as protect them by giving them empowering information that can become crucial to their professional and personal success. Of course, going to work abroad anywhere requires somewhat of an adventurous personality, and I believe that there are people who need just a little push to realize that they have this personality within. I also hope that after reading this book and the conversations it contains, this adventurous side will certainly begin to shine through.

Always remember, there is nothing more fulfilling than to spend at least a year abroad, living and working in a foreign culture and doing something influential. What better way is there to influence than to teach. Anyone with the right attitude, motivation, and experience can teach in South Korea.

Chapter 1:
A New Beginning

How and why I chose Korea as a working ground

For a few months before I decided to teach abroad, I was in a really good situation. I had just bought a home in the California desert. A home I dreamed about buying just one year before, and that I worked very hard to get. I then spent about $16,000 gutting it out and remodeling it into something beautiful. I had also just graduated from my university with a master's degree, in which during two years of studying for, I never thought I'd achieve. My life was going well, and with my new degree, I was confident that I would be able to find a good job near my new home and continue living comfortably and quietly. Little did I realize how much the political turmoil my country (the U.S.A) was involved in, in terms of the war in Iraq and the re-election of an already scrutinized president, would affect the single most important thing I needed to do at that time: find a job.

For three months I sat in front of my computer, searching for jobs, submitting my resume and researching companies. There came a point early on in those three months when I realized that I should no longer limit my applications to those jobs related to my field of study. So, I began applying for even the most menial and unskilled positions, like dollar store clerks and delivery drivers. I frantically searched and applied, and all the while, the bills kept coming in. The credit cards I used to charge my whopping $16,000 worth of home remodeling services and supplies were starting to come around and bite me hard. I panicked. I had to think about what to do before my life turned into a debt disaster... again. I kept thinking, *why was it* so difficult to find a simple job, especially with my experience and education? I was a newly graduated anthropologist, dammit! It should have been easier than that! Then I realized that I wasn't the only one with this problem. The political events that involved my country at that time, as well as the threat of local terrorism, were damaging the economy, and it was evident in the country's job market. The job situation was tough, and many educated and qualified people (along with many non-educated people) had a hard time finding work. I suppose it didn't help that I now lived in a small, desert community, far away from major businesses and higher-end jobs.

After two and a half months, and in the midst of my panic, I surrendered to what I believed was the last resort. No, not welfare; a job overseas. I did what I never imagined I would have to do. I began applying for the only type of overseas jobs that I felt I was qualified for. English teaching positions in Asia.

Why Asia? I'll explain. During my online job research, I found that even though I did not possess teaching certification, credentials, or a PhD, I was still qualified to teach English there. Whereas in the United States, I could not teach English (ESL) without at least a TESL certification (Teaching English as a Second Language) and academic experience in the subject. Also, teaching at the University level in the United States usually requires a PhD. The teaching requirements in the U.S.A can be stringent compared to other countries, making it impossible for me to find this sort of job unless I travel abroad. Of course, I was also qualified to teach in many other areas of the world and not just Asia.

However, I admit that I also have always been fascinated with Asia, especially East Asia. It has always been a land of exoticism to me. I had the wonderful opportunity to travel to Japan just two years before, and I loved every moment of it. At that time, I started to become interested in Confucianism and the Eastern way of life. Thinking about working in this land of exoticism just fueled the fire for me and I started to become more positive about my overseas job search. I began to think that taking advantage of the opportunity to teach in Asia would perhaps have several advantages for me: First, it would give me a chance to learn more about the region. Second, the teaching salaries listed were impressive, allowing me to save more than I would if I had a similar job in my own country. Third, I assumed that international work experience would look excellent on my resume, hopefully working to my advantage when I would return to the U.S.A and look for a job. Fourth, I would *finally* be employed. As I poked through all the English teaching recruiting agencies and researched jobs and contracts, I noticed that the countries that seemed to have the highest demand for native English speakers were China, Japan and Korea. The job selections in these countries were greater and I could be pickier when applying for them. All of the contracts from these three countries seemed attractive in one way or another, and most importantly, I was qualified for most of them. Eventually, after many hours of scrutinizing, I began to limit my job search to South Korea only.

China's teaching contracts were attractive in terms of teaching hours and were similar to Japan's contracts in that the employers provided housing, vacation time, and health insurance. However, the teacher's salary in China was substantially lower than Japan's, sometimes more than half. Of course, the cost of living in China is extremely low. The average teacher's salary in China of $750 per month can take you far and last you a very long time while living there. However, if your purpose is to remit money to your own country (assuming it is the U.S.A., Canada, Great Britain, Australia, or any other Western nation), $750 can be pocket change. Taking a job in China would defeat my main purpose of paying off high credit card bills. The salary I would make wouldn't even cover the minimum monthly payments on my credit cards.

Japan's teaching contracts had the same basic set-up as China's contracts in that the employers provided housing, vacation time, and health insurance. However, the salaries offered in the Japanese contracts were more than double the Chinese contracts. Japan's contracts were impressive. I did find some contracts that required the teacher to contribute toward rent. That may have been because the rents in Japan are painfully high. In my opinion, those contracts are never good deals, unless you are making an extra-added bonus salary to cover your rent each month. Aside from other impressive offers the Japanese contracts boasted, it was important to remember that the cost of living in Japan is amazingly high—it is one of the most expensive countries in the world. I remembered my trip to Japan several years before and how expensive it was just to eat a bowl of Ramen at a restaurant. And since my objective was to pay bills and save money, I didn't want to worry about having to spend my hard-earned salary on food, transportation and high utility costs.

Korea's teaching contracts, on the other hand, had the best of both worlds as far as the employer providing housing, vacation time, and health insurance. The salaries were also identical to the salaries that the Japanese contracts offered—which were very impressive. Through my research, the only difference between working in Korea and working in Japan was that the cost of living in Korea was much lower. One can eat an entire meal at a Korean restaurant for three to five dollars (U.S.), and an intra-city bus ride only costs eighty cents to a dollar depending on the distance travelled. Income taxes in Korea are currently approximately 3.5 percent of one's total salary, meaning that virtually everything I would make could be saved or used to pay my bills. In Korea, I wouldn't have to worry about astronomically high rent, transportation costs, and grocery bills like I would in Japan. Overall, taking a Korean teaching contract was, by far, the most common-sense thing to do.

So, the story goes. Over the two and a half years I have spent teaching in Korea at six different institutions, I have rarely regretted my decision to go there. The few times that I did regret, I had been experiencing a bit of culture-shock and homesickness. This has always passed. It has been a cultural roller coaster ride from beginning to end, but nevertheless, an adventure. Just like any other expatriate in Korea, I had a ton of good, bad, exciting, confusing, and frustrating times, but in the end, the experience itself was worth it. I can't say I would want to spend many years living and working in South Korea, but I *can* say that many people do. Many expatriates have been teaching English in South Korea for years. Some have been teaching for ten or fifteen years, others for only two or three. Of course, if you've never had the experience of living abroad, particularly in Asia, I recommended that you stick to the cities where things are familiar to you. Living for the first time in the Asian countryside can bring a lot of culture-shock and hardship, especially when you hold things like McDonald's, shopping malls, and socializing with Westerners dear to your heart. Trust me, I have lived in the big cities and the itty-bitty towns where I spent days dreaming of holding a Hershey's Bar.

Is Korea for You?

Sounds like this adventure is fit for you? This book is a guide for people who are thinking about wandering outside of the comfortable confines of their own country to become an expatriate and teach English. This book is also a cultural glimpse of what to **expect when living** and working abroad, particularly in South Korea, as well as learning how to deal with cultural differences in the classroom and a new physical and social environment. I have included not only my own insight, interpretations, and advice, but also other expatriates', all who share the common thread of being English teachers. The stories they share are incredibly valuable to anyone interested in culture, travel and working abroad. I hope that this book will provide an abundance of insight on how Western expatriates fit in Korean society, a homogenous society that has only been truly open to the rest of the world for a little over fifty years. Finally, and most importantly, I hope that this book will provide sufficient advice on what and what not to do (and what and what not to sign) when considering a teaching career in South Korea.

Once you've decided to take that job in South Korea, there are mainly two ways you can pick up and move. First, you can carefully plan everything—store most of your personal belongings in public storage, hire a company to ship the rest, and most importantly, meticulously pack the things that you know you could never find at the local market in your new host country. OR, you can chuck everything in the trash—every piece of clothing and ridiculous knick-knack—and pack only what you consider vital to life in two or three suitcases, and just bail. Recently, I did the latter. As a result, I felt liberated. I was finally free of all those little stupid things I used to spend hours adjusting and rearranging. What good would they have done me in Korea anyway? The things I filled my two suitcases with were the things I could never let go of... pictures of my dogs, my boyfriend and family, CD's and several books, clothing for work, and my video camera and computer which happen to be sentimental gifts. When I finally arrived to Korea, I realized that a 'lack of stuff' is the most stress-relieving condition I could possibly have! This liberation accompanied my adventurous character very well. If you're the kind that has an adventurous character and is highly adaptable, it's best to experience things without all your needless 'stuff'. All of that will just weigh you down.

Chapter 2:
Know Before You Go: Understanding the stats and facts

The E2 Teaching Visa

A visa is a kind of certificate or stamp that gives a traveler permission to enter a country and stay for a designated amount of time. Types of visas vary (work visa, business, tourist, etc.), as do the times allowed to remain in the country.

According to statistics published by the Korean immigration bureau, in 2008 a total of 38,822 E2 teaching visas were granted. The majority of these visa holders came (and still come) from the United States, the United Kingdom, Ireland, Canada, Australia, New Zealand and South Africa. The remaining E2 visa holders came from France, Italy, Germany, Japan and China. Although the majority of E2 visa holders teach a language (mostly English), there are other professions that are granted this type of visa. For the purpose of this book, whenever an 'E2 visa holder' is mentioned, I am referring to an individual who is working as an English teacher. The embassy/consulate of your country (in Korea) should have information posted on their website regarding visas, contracts, and other useful information you should review before deciding to take a teaching job. The United States Embassy Korea website is http://seoul.usembassy.gov.

Below is a chart that puts immigration in perspective. Table 1.1 shows the total number of individuals by country who have entered South Korea in 2008. Beside the totals, the chart details how many of those individuals have gotten E2 teaching visas. Table 1.2 shows the total number of E2 visas issued to individuals of all countries between 2004 and 2007. Notice that the number of E2 visas granted have steadily increased by the thousands every year since 2004. This data indicates that the need for foreign teachers is increasing, and as a result of this, Korea is becoming a little more ethnically diverse and global.

Table 1.1 is especially important in that it demonstrates the likelihood of meeting other foreign individuals during your time living and working in Korea. For example, the likelihood of you meeting someone from the United States (teaching or not) is much higher than the likelihood of you meeting someone from Ireland, regardless of which part of Korea you live in. If you come to Korea from Ireland to teach, and you are looking for the company of other Irish English teachers, the outlook is grim considering only 692 Irish had E2 teaching visas in 2008. In comparison, 11,060 Canadians were teaching English in Korea in 2008. So, if you're Canadian and are looking for the company of your fellow countrymen, you're in luck! You may end up having a lot of Canadian English teachers working alongside you.

Table 1.1 Total E2 Visa holders by country compared to the total entering South Korea in 2008

Region	Total entering the country on various visas and statuses	Total E2 visa holders
United States	644, 012	17, 184 (10,013 m, 7,171 f)
Canada	95, 993	11, 060 (5,544 m, 5,516 f)
United Kingdom	82, 093	3, 386 (2,181 m, 1,205 f)
Ireland	6, 404	692 (426 m, 266 f)
South Africa	6, 108	1, 569 (680 m, 889 f)
Australia	91, 801	1, 239 (719 m, 520 f)
New Zealand	23, 809	1, 260 (736 m, 524 f)
Total	950, 220	36, 390 (20,299 m, 16,091 f)

Table 1.2 Total E2 Visa by year

Year	Total E2 visas issued to individuals of all countries
2004	23, 134
2005	25, 014
2006	29, 263
2007	35, 457
2008 (most recent stats available)	**38, 822**

Melissa Christine Karpinski

How Do I Get a Visa to Teach?

As previously mentioned, and further emphasized on the Korean Consulate General in Los Angeles website, in order to get an English instructor status in South Korea you will definitely need to obtain an E-2 visa. In order to obtain the E-2 visa, you will need to have at least a bachelors degree (or equivalent) and a valid passport. You must also be a citizen of one of the major English speaking countries (USA, UK, Canada, New Zealand, Australia, Ireland and South Africa). When applying for the visa, you must submit a visa application form with a current passport sized photo. According to the revised Korean immigration laws, a visa interview is now required. My other half had to undergo this interview and it was a very basic interview in which they asked him why he wanted to work in Korea. Your employer will also have to obtain a visa number for you from his/her local immigration office and you must give that number to the Korean consulate in your home country where you are applying for the visa. The following part is especially important: you must obtain a criminal background check from your local police station and have that certificate notarized. It's best to ask a notary to meet you at the police station so he/she can have it notarized in front of the station staff member. Once it is notarized, you must submit it to the Secretary of State's office to have it 'apostillized'[7]. This is a French word that means 'to have certified'. This process can take up to two weeks, so be sure to provide adequate time for this to be done before your flight departure date. This will need to be submitted to the Korean immigration office for processing of your visa (along with everything else; visa application, original diploma, sealed transcripts, photos, resume, and signed employment contract). If you are working through a recruiter, it is the recruiter's job to collect all of these documents from you and submit them to have your visa number processed so that you can obtain your visa. In the past, it was possible for first time E2 visa applicants to come to Korea first and then hop over to Japan to obtain the visa. Now, with more stringent immigration rules, it is no longer possible to receive your first E2 visa in Japan. You must get it in your home country. However, if you want to renew after your first year, then you can renew in Japan. The renewal in Tokyo, Osaka, or Fukuoka saves you from a very expensive trip back home. Recently (2008-2009), immigration has renewed visas for foreign English instructors without requiring them to even leave Korea. When I switched to a new employer after my most recent contract was finished, immigration simply renewed my visa for another year after I paid the fee. I didn't have to leave the country at all. It may depend on what situation you're in. Immigration has been known to change policies on the fly, so it's best to check with them periodically for any updates once you're in Korea.

    The requirements for Canadians to obtain an E2 visa to work in Korea are exactly the same as Americans. Canadians must submit the same materials. Two small differences are turnaround time and cost. The Consulate General of Korea in Toronto website (http://www.koreanconsulate.on.ca/en/) lists a 5-10 day processing time for visas, whereas the Consulate General of Korea in Los Angeles will process it in just a few days. Of course, this is assuming you already have your visa number in hand. At the time of this writing, the visa fee in the United States is approximately $45 and in Canada approximately $55.

If your place of origin is Australia, New Zealand, or the United Kingdom, it's best to confirm with the Korean Consulate in your area what the visa requirements for you will be.

Chapter 3:
A Long Way from Home:
Your New Environment and the Culture Around You

An Anxious Start

The first time I accepted a job in Korea, I took a fourteen hour flight direct from Los Angeles to Seoul. During the flight, I was so nervous that something wouldn't go right, perhaps I would get lost or the director of the school wouldn't come and pick me up. However, for not knowing what to expect, all went very smoothly. The job that I took was for an English kindergarten. I understood my contract well, but I didn't know much about the area, the students, or the staff I would be working with. Of course, this alone made me a bit nervous. Not knowing anyone who I could get advice from, I had no choice but to go with the flow. During my first week, I was in bliss. I really had a great time orienting myself with my brand new world. The staff and the foreign teachers at my new school (two from the States and one from Canada) helped me a great deal with getting settled into my new apartment, finding my way around, and showing me the ropes so to speak. They had become an excellent support structure and were always there when I needed them the most.

    The city where I took my first teaching job was called Cheonan City. It was a very diverse city that had a variety of city styles rolled into one; eclectic, modern, traditional, countryside and concrete. It was a huge city with about 800,000 people, and it had (and still has) a centralized downtown with a surrounding suburban area. Of course very few things were in English! If you live and work in any city other than Seoul (the capital) and you don't speak any Korean, it can be a bit challenging to get around. Sometimes, you can run into a kind English-speaking person who is gracious enough to help you if you are at the store or a restaurant. Most people are very helpful to foreigners, however, if you live in the ultra-countryside as I did when I took my second contract, you may run into a problem with Koreans being timid or embarrassed to use their English with foreigners. They will tend to shy away from you if you attempt to speak to them. Of course, it is always a good idea to learn some basic phrases in Korean so that you won't have a problem getting around, ordering food, and expressing things that you need. After you've learned some simple phrases, it is also a good idea to learn how to read Hangul (Korean alphabet). It is very easy to learn Hangul and can even be mastered within a week.

I didn't speak basic Korean well or read Hangul at all until I came back to Korea for my second year and my third teaching contract. I came to a small town called Jincheon City. Although, it wasn't a city at all, but just a town with a population of about seventy-thousand. This town was (and still is) a single step above total and complete countryside. Full of farmers, English was nonexistent, and there were only a few other English-speaking teachers. It was in Jincheon that I really pressed myself to learn more Korean and get the reading down-pat. I had no other choice. I needed to communicate, and it occurred to me immediately that there was a very slim chance I could use any English to communicate. This town wasn't like Cheonan City, where I would occasionally run into English speakers and English street signs. This was much more foreign to me. As if Cheonan City wasn't unfamiliar enough! My time in Jincheon City, as lonely as it often was, benefitted my Korean language and reading skills a great deal. Of course, it's the students that often deserve the credit. They have always been my Korean teachers, since it was them I had to learn to communicate with. They will be your teachers as well, and learning basic phrases of Korean will come naturally as long as you are dealing with kids and beginner students.

Understanding Collectivism in Korea

Many Westerners I spoke to in Korea expressed the viewpoint that Korean people were so collective in many ways. In a sense this is true, and in a sense this is not true. Clothing style was (and still is) very conservative, although if you travel to the more cosmopolitan cities, like Seoul, fashion conservativeness dwindles. Exposing bare backs and too much skin is certainly not common and will warrant a lot of stares in a small town. Wild hairstyles, sassy piercings, and tattoos rarely seem to exist. When I went to Osaka, Japan to get my work visa early on in my first contract, (even though Japanese are also considered collective) young people had a strong sense of individuality in the way they behaved, the way they dressed, and the way their overall appearance was. Of course, this opinion is solely based on my observations.

Korea is influenced by their surrounding neighbors (China and Japan) in terms of fashion and popular culture, and now more than ever, it is influenced by the West as well. Sometimes this influence is very apparent and sometimes it's not. As a Westerner being introduced to a collective society, it is possible for Western expatriates to become extremely frustrated with Korean cultural customs and behavior. This frustration not only includes what they perceive as 'lack of individuality and independence', but also includes other very minute cultural differences. Collectivism involves participating in actions that benefit the entire group, while individualism involves participating in actions that benefit the self or individual alone. The West is certainly an individualistic society, whereas the Far East is collectivist. Often in the Korean workplace, the nail that sticks out gets hammered down. If you're familiar with this phrase, this is enough said. If you're not, elaboration may be needed. As an employee in a Korean workplace, I was expected to not question authority, not ask too many questions, and to conform to the rest of the staff. One person's decisions had the ability to affect everyone else in the office. Conforming to the character of my surroundings, in my opinion, often impeded my creative urges and 'outside the box' ideas that I sometimes passionately wanted to execute. Of course, this unspoken rule of conformity was to simply keep the harmony in the office and not make waves. I understand that this is a cultural way of life, and as a Westerner, I found it important to find a way to adapt to this kind of office lifestyle, and at the same time, allow my individual and creative urges to shine through. I have managed to find a happy balance, although sometimes at the expense of being jokingly labeled a rogue English teacher. Many institutions of learning in Korea are now trying to change this 'collectivist' environment and encourage its Western (and Korean) staff to think creatively and independently. My most recent job tried dearly to encourage its staff to think outside the box. When you begin teaching in a Korean classroom it is important to feel your way through the office character and employee culture and make informed and intelligent decisions regarding your behavior, your level of inquisitiveness, and your drive to throw out new ideas. You must decide if your place of work can handle and appreciate your individuality. Unfortunately, workplace culture cannot be fully understood until after you've worked in the school for a few weeks to a few months. By then, the contract has already been signed. Make your best judgment of the school and the people around you if you have the opportunity to be interviewed, introduced to the staff, and taken on a tour of the school.

The Do's and Don'ts of Housing

While searching for a teaching job in Korea, one of the most important things to consider is what kind of housing the school or institution is offering you. Almost one hundred percent of the time the school will provide housing free of charge. If you choose to find your own housing, which is becoming more common with English teachers fed up with studio apartments, the school will often provide a monthly housing allowance to help you pay for rent. Usually this housing allowance is small—about three-hundred dollars (U.S.), or the monthly cost of a studio apartment. Of course, this depends on where you live. If you will live in Seoul, your housing allowance may be much bigger since housing is more expensive there. However, it's either or. You will not receive both the provided housing and the allowance. The housing that a hagwon or public school normally provides is a studio apartment complete with a kitchenette and a separate bathroom. It is small, perhaps one hundred and twenty square feet. Of course, you will live there alone. Any school that requires you to share a studio apartment with another teacher is a bad set up. It's a red flag for things to come: disorganization and crowded conditions.

Sometimes, you will have two bedroom shared housing offered to you in which you would share an apartment with one or two other foreign teachers. Be sure to ask what utility bills you will be responsible for and what the average cost of them is for both the winter and summer. Normally, you would be responsible for gas, electric, cable T.V., and internet if you choose to have it. The gas is usually required for cooking and the electric is required for heating and air conditioning. My gas and electric bills were often about twenty to thirty dollars (U.S.) a month. My cable T.V. was satellite, and it cost twenty-seven dollars (U.S.) per month. My internet was high speed cable and it was also twenty-seven dollars (U.S.) per month. Expect to pay around one-hundred dollars (U.S.) for bills, possibly more in the winter since heating is expensive.

The apartment rental system in Korea is certainly not the same like what I am used to in the United States. In Korea, if you rent an apartment you have to pay what's called 'key money'. It is a deposit that depends on the size of the apartment and monthly rental amount. Sometimes, the more 'key money' that is paid, the lower the monthly rent can be. Conversely, the less 'key money' that is paid, the higher the monthly rent can be. Fortunately, you will not have to worry about paying any 'key money' since the school director pays this for you. That is why school directors often place their teachers in studio apartments. They can pay a small amount of 'key money' as well as pay cheap rent, *and* keep flexible and short leases. Bringing a foreign teacher to their school requires a lot of expenses as well as visa fees (pension contributions, round trip airfare, and severance pay), so school directors want to keep other costs down as much as possible, including apartment costs. Of course, other housing can be obtained, especially if you work in Seoul. Many Real Estate Agencies are now working with foreigners to find them adequate housing. You can try and find your own apartment (especially if you plan on bringing family or pets) and just accept the monthly housing allowance your school offers. Beware! Housing can be expensive in certain areas of Korea! A two bedroom, nine-hundred square foot apartment that I would normally pay twelve-hundred dollars (U.S.) a month for in Southern California can cost between two-thousand and three-thousand dollars (U.S.) in upper-class areas of Seoul! If you end up working in an upper-class area, it's best to share the housing with house-mates or other teachers, because the three-hundred dollar housing allowance your school will provide to you will only cover a fraction of the rent if you get a big place. Also, don't forget about the 'key money'. If you choose your own apartment (and it is expensive) then your employer may not want to pay the entire 'key money' required. The key money for a three-thousand dollar-a-month apartment can burn your wallet—around five-thousand to ten-thousand dollars (U.S.) extra, sometimes more depending on the area and the place. If you plan to live solo, take the studio (or one bedroom) that is offered by the school, it's rent-free and the bills are cheap!

During my third contract, housing was the biggest issue. When I began searching for another teaching job in Korea (while I was still in the States) I had plans to take my two big dogs and my lovely cat along with me. I had a Doberman mix and a Shepherd mix. However, I was concerned about their freedom and happiness in Korea, and I didn't want to stick them in a small studio apartment. As I worked through a teacher recruiting agency, I was very specific about finding a job that would provide housing for me and my three pets. I was very firm on requesting either a small Korean home with a garden, or a 2 bedroom apartment near a park where I could allow my dogs to run around and play. I was willing to accept a slightly lower salary in exchange for my requested housing, only as a vehicle to motivate the school directors to consider me. I knew that finding this kind of housing would be tough and finding a school director that was willing to pay me well *and* pay for larger accommodations would be even tougher.

I had to remain flexible in terms of the city and area I lived and worked in. Nevertheless, the recruiter put me in contact with a school director in Jincheon City, about 2 hours south of Seoul. She was having a difficult time finding a foreign teacher who wanted to live and work at her academy in the countryside, so she was willing to consider my request. After a little bit of negotiation we came to a good deal. I accepted one-hundred dollars (U.S.) less than the salary offered, and in exchange I was promised larger accommodations for me and my dogs. After a few months of my director trying to pull some strings in the town, I got really lucky and received a nice little three bedroom mobile home on a country road with a half-acre of fenced land where my dogs could run and play. It ended up being a very good deal, and worth sacrificing one-hundred dollars-a-month—at least until wintertime! When wintertime came, my heating bills went through the roof because the mobile home walls were thin! That was something I did not take into consideration when accepting the home. Overall, it was beneficial to me and my dogs. Of course, don't expect to find a deal like this easily. If you are traveling and working alone (without family or animals), directors will be reluctant to honor your request for bigger housing simply because you don't need it. Most Koreans live simple and small. Many of my child students even sleep in the same bedroom with their parents and brothers and sisters simply because they only have small one or two bedroom apartments. In all honesty, even though I survived in Korea with my pets, I don't recommend that you bring them. The flight is a huge added cost and cities are bustling with fast cars and people who are actually fearful of bigger dogs. Your living and apartment choices will be severely limited and it's not fun having to walk your dogs to the local park in freezing winter weather.

Chapter 4:
Getting the Job You Want

Choices, Choices: Public School, University, or Hagwon

My most recent teaching job was at a public elementary school, and it was by-far the best. My other half works in a graduate school which is about the same as a university. Of course, I cannot share personal experiences of teaching at a university because I have never done so, but I can tell you how the hours, contract, students, rules and basic work environment differ between elementary schools, hagwons, and universities. Also, in the 'Conversations' section of this book, I have included a conversation I had with a friend who is a middle school teacher. Middle school is equivalent to a 'junior high' in the U.S.A.

A hagwon is basically a cram school for elementary, middle, and high school students where they can learn new subjects or enhance their learning of subjects already taught in their day schools. Parents pay tuition for their children to attend these hagwons and children often go to several different ones per day. There are foreign language, math, science, art, tae-kwon-do, sports, dance (fine arts), and study hagwons, just to name a few. English hagwons are extremely popular given the high demand for learning English. This is why native English speakers have an array of teaching jobs to choose from. Parents are flocking to enroll their children into English schools, especially schools that have native English speakers. Hagwons can sometimes be a little chaotic to work for. There are a lot of children of all different ages, and it is difficult to place them exactly according to their English proficiency. An

English teacher can run into the problem of having slightly different levels of students in one class (as well as different age groups). Because of the gender and age separation practiced among children in Korean culture, this situation is not simple to deal with. Children definitely do not often become friends with children older or younger than they are, and boys certainly do not cooperate with girls in a classroom. Of course, there are exceptions. I always found that my nine to eleven-year-olds cared less about gender and age in the classroom than the children younger or older than them. If you teach at a hagwon it's a good idea to be extremely flexible with dealing with a variety of levels, attitudes, and changes in times and schedules. Remember this!

A positive point with working at a hagwon are the hours. Since hagwons are characteristically after-school academies (English hagwons in particular), students don't start rolling through the door until the afternoon. That means the teachers don't have to be at work until the afternoon as well. My first contract was with an English kindergarten, so I started my day at 10:00 am. However, the kindergarten transformed into a hagwon after the morning. This is when the regular day students went home and the English elementary students arrived in the afternoon. Unfortunately, my day at that school ran rather late, until 5:00 p.m. My third contract, however, was with a true English hagwon that didn't open until around 2:00 p.m. So, my day started at 12:30 in which I was contracted out to a few companies in the area to teach employees, then I would come back to the school around 2:00 to teach English to children until 7:00. Those hours were perfect for me and the lifestyle I had. It was wonderful because I bypassed any morning rush, I didn't have to wake up early, and I could do the things I loved every morning, like walk my dogs and exercise. I still got off at a reasonable hour after work, again, bypassing the afternoon rush and spending time with friends until late. I didn't have to be in bed early and I didn't have to wake up early. The schedule was the best I had ever had. If you're not a morning person, I recommend taking a job like this.

If you work for a public elementary or middle school, however, your day will certainly begin a lot earlier. It is the closest to a standard 9-5 schedule. It will be perhaps even 7-4. Since English is supplementary in a hagwon, you wouldn't normally keep track of grades, report cards, and achieving any type of standards. If this is done at all, it would be completed by the Korean staff. However, the opposite is true when you teach in a public school. Expect bigger classes with more students (even though they will fall into the same age groups but not necessarily the same levels), a ton of report cards to complete, preparing tests and adequate homework, et-cetera, et-cetera. If you are the type of person who enjoys more organization and cares about keeping track of students' progress (and boosting and improving your professional teaching career), perhaps the public school route is the better way to go. The curriculum is certainly a lot more organized, and since you are an employee of a public institution, you are sure to have very good benefits, great healthcare, all holidays off, and adequate vacation time. Also, you have less chance of being cheated by the director since you're getting paid by the government, not by a single individual who controls the entire school bank account. Of course, situations vary. There is always a risk of obtaining a job where you are taken advantage of. That is why it is important to cover all of your bases, talk to people, and do the research necessary before signing a contract.

If you're a more experienced teacher, have a master's degree, and TESOL or CELTA certification, you can get a university or graduate school job. Universities offer excellent teaching hours (often a lot less than hagwons and public middle, elementary, or high schools) and long vacations. There are quite a few very good universities that offer four to five months in a row paid vacation every year. Even the jobs that offer two months paid vacation sound juicy to me. Expect, however, to spend a lot of time planning and preparing for classes. Of course, you will have to consider the extra office hours into your teaching schedule when looking at university teaching job postings. Usually the posting will mention the required weekly (or monthly) office hours. If it doesn't, ask about it. Universities will also offer excellent benefits including health care and a retirement account. My other half teaches at a graduate school in Seoul in which the director even throws in a free gym membership. Housing offered will be the same as a public children's school or hagwon. You may even be asked to live in on-campus housing (maybe even a dormitory). If you are the type of person who works better with adults who care about learning and you are responsible enough to get your classroom planning and office work done, then the university route would be the way to go. Remember, teaching at a university is for teachers who already have experience teaching and who have a master's degree from an accredited institution. You don't necessarily need a TESOL or CELTA certificate, but it can help a great deal. I know because my other half was offered two different university positions based on his CELTA certification (and one of them based on the recommendation of his CELTA instructor). The better school accepted him based on the certification and the recommendation in lieu of the master's degree. This situation, however, is rare. There are a few universities that will press for TESOL or CELTA certification, however, a master's degree is a well-known requirement for teaching at a university. A bachelor's degree is the only requirement for teaching at a public children's school or a hagwon.

The fact is, English positions are everywhere. Whether they're at hagwons, kindergartens, or universities, jobs for Westerners are in the thousands. The important thing is to select the one that's best suitable for you and that you are most qualified for.

What Qualifications Do You Need?

Aside from requiring that English be your native language, every Korean school requires foreign English teachers to have at least a bachelor's degree from an accredited institution to teach. As previously stated, universities require a master's degree and some universities ask that you have a few years teaching experience at a university level and/or TESOL or CELTA certification. If your plan is to work in a public or private children's school, you won't need much, if any, experience at all. If you do not possess a bachelor's degree and a school wants to hire you anyway, you should see that as a red flag! It is illegal for foreigners to teach English in Korea without a degree, and if you do it, you will not be able to obtain an E2 visa. Teaching without a visa is extremely risky. When I started at my first school in Cheonan City my visa was still being processed the first day I started work. So, I was officially working in Korea illegally for about thirty days before my employer sent me to Japan to seal the visa deal. Of course, I didn't know this. I thought it was standard practice for teachers to begin working and then obtain their visa at a later date. We had three other foreign English teachers who started at about the same time I did at this school and two of them didn't have their visas yet as well. I remember hearing from a co-worker that immigration made a surprise visit one day to the school and the director quickly scooped up the teachers without a visa and ushered them out the back door. He urged them to keep quiet until the inspectors left. Of course, I've heard a few other horror stories. I heard that one director at a different school told his teachers to wait on the ledge outside a second story window when immigration showed up. I can't help but believe this is true considering the fear I've seen in hagwon directors' eyes when the issue of immigration and possible fines comes up. Ironically, after a few months of working in Cheonan City, as I was walking home with my co-workers after work, a black van pulled up alongside of us and out jumped several immigration inspectors. They immediately asked to see our passports to check if we had valid visas! Of course, there is no reason for you to be fearful of immigration or working in Korea. The circumstances I've described are extreme and not to be worried about as long as you obtain your visa before beginning work.

There is conflicting information in the English teaching community about the workings of Korean immigration in Korea. Some say that they are strict and feared and swift to deport any foreigner who doesn't follow the rules. Others say that they really don't care and don't put much of an effort in trying to find and deport illegal English teachers (such as individuals who are giving private English lessons or who don't have proper work visas). I have reason to believe that it depends on where you live. You are more likely a needle in a haystack if you live in a big city, so your actions are less likely to be closely followed. Generally, I believe that the latter is true: immigration doesn't put much effort in trying to pinpoint and deport foreigners who don't follow the rules. There is simply not enough manpower to worry about every foreign English teacher and what he is doing every moment in Korea. However, it's always best to not take any chances. As I mentioned earlier, I had a run-in with an immigration van packed with a few immigration officials who decided to give my co-workers and I a hard time on that particular day. That was the only time I had ever had someone question my status in Korea. I never had any problems after that and there were many times when I *should* have been questioned. Also, throughout my entire time living and working in Korea, I had known English teachers who were teaching privately (which is illegal in Korea), and who had multiple jobs for many years under a single work visa (also illegal), and they had never been questioned at any time by immigration officials.

The Advantage and Disadvantage of Using a Job Recruiter

It's no secret that there is an enormous demand for English language education in Korea, and it will be apparent immediately if you look on overseas employment websites, such as the popular DavesEslCafe.com. Using a recruiter can be very helpful if you are planning on working in a hagwon or public/private elementary, middle or high school. Recruiters are not normally used if you're looking for a university or graduate school position. There are thousands of schools looking for foreign English teaching staff and hundreds of recruiters catering to them. It is the recruiter's job to find what you are looking for. Don't be afraid to ask questions and be specific with what you want regarding age of children, city you want to work in, and acceptable pay. Of course, you must remain realistic and reasonable. You cannot ask the recruiter to find you a job with an unusually higher than average salary if you lack the credentials to apply for it. The average salary right now is approximately two-million to 2.2 million won for all schools, which translates into fifteen-hundred to seventeen-hundred dollars (U.S.). Some schools offer less and some offer more. If you want the maximum, you must select a school that is offering the maximum. Of course, if you have extra credentials that warrant higher than average pay, the salary is usually negotiable. Again, don't be afraid to be specific with the recruiter as to exactly what kind of salary you are looking for. Job recruiters are paid a lot of money by school directors to find them the right teacher — usually about fifteen-hundred to two-thousand dollars (U.S.). That is why a recruiter is highly motivated to find you a job and place you in it right away. Just beware of a recruiter that is rushing to place you with disregard for your wants and needs. This person is probably trying to dump you so he can collect his commission and move on to the next client. If this happens, move on to a different recruiter who is more attentive to both you and the school director. This person should work with you and be in contact with you for the duration of your contract as well as always be available for any questions you might have.

There are plenty of advantages to using a job recruiter, especially if you will be working in Korea for the first time. A job recruiter has access to schools and can communicate with the directors easily. They are the go-between for you and the potential school. This mainly helps you in two ways: it takes away the stress from having to communicate with multiple directors who may not speak English too well, and it simplifies the entire paperwork and application process. Instead of applying to schools directly and sending a dozen copies of your diplomas, transcripts and resumes, you just send one certified set of everything straight to the recruiter. The recruiter then provides copies of these things to the schools you want to apply to. When you decide on the job you want, the recruiter submits the originals to the school. Overall, using a recruiter makes things easy and quick. Since your recruiter should speak English well, there can be no miscommunications about your job wants and needs. As aforementioned, a recruiter also has *access*; this is something you don't have as a first-time job seeker in Korea. He or she can contact *any* school in the country in search of a position for you.

Another excellent advantage to using a recruiter is that if you ever have a problem with your school or director in terms of communication, pay, benefits, or labor law, the recruiter can help. They are knowledgeable about contracts, what's good and bad, what's legal and illegal, and if they can't immediately give you an answer on these issues, they are to do the research and find out. Unfortunately, there are some dishonest school directors out there, and some try to cheat their foreign staff by twisting the language in the contract or delaying pay or benefits. If they know you are in contact with your recruiter regarding these issues, directors are less likely to take advantage of you. They know they can be blacklisted or reported to the government or labor inspectors.

Some schools, however, may not be able to afford a recruiter, making your access to that school nonexistent. Although, given the success of English language schools in Korea, I can't imagine many schools being financially insufficient to be able to pay a recruiter's fee, unless the school is brand new with low enrollment or in a very small town catering to an extremely small or poor community. In this case, the school may try to advertise for foreign teaching staff on its own (newspapers, websites, and word of mouth). In this case, you might never see the advertisement.

It's not a good idea to use a recruiter if you are looking for a university position. Recruiters won't even help you if they know you are limiting your search to university jobs. You must apply to the university directly and send each university an application packet complete with copies of diplomas, transcripts, resume, cover letter, passport and photos. The hiring process for universities tends to be very organized and professional, and they are not in need of a recruiter to find them foreign staff. If you apply to a university, you are on your own in terms of negotiating pay and making deals.

There are some disadvantages to using a recruiter. As I mentioned before, some recruiters try to hastily place you with little regard to your wants and needs, just so they can collect their commission and move on. It's difficult to spot these bad recruiters so it's best to work with several at the same time so you can compare how hard they work for you and how well they listen. My last recruiter promised details that were supposed to be in my contract, however, they ended up being miswritten or omitted entirely! For example, my last recruiter informed me that my job start time would be 11:00 a.m. and finish time would be 5:00 p.m. But when the contract was presented to me for signing, it listed a much earlier start time and a much later finish time! I was confused, and the school staff was confused as well, since they never told the recruiter that the hours were 11:00 – 5:00. There were also some details that were not communicated correctly to the school. For example, I specified to the recruiter to communicate to the school that I did not want to contribute any part of my pay to the national pension. He told me that he had checked with the school and it would not be a problem. I would not have to contribute. Later, when I received my first pay deposit, I noticed that the pension had been deducted. When I asked the pay staff if my recruiter communicated the 'pension request' to them, they said he did no such thing, and I had no choice but to pay it. It was utterly frustrating. After much arguing, the school finally granted my request to not have a pension deduction. It was a major fault of my recruiter. He seemed to fail at communicating the simplest of things. This same recruiter also reassured me that the commute time to my school would be no more than twenty minutes. I should have dropped him immediately after I did a test commute to the school and the time ended up being an hour and a half! These were lessons learned. Double and triple check everything your recruiter says. Be sure to confirm all the details with him/her, especially anything regarding your contract. If your recruiter doesn't speak English well, move on to the next one immediately.

Chapter 5:
Surviving Korean Culture

Perceptions of the Other

My eight year old student looked at me one afternoon and exclaimed, "my mommy said that you are soooooo pretty!" I didn't know what to say. It was at an inappropriate time while I was reading a story about a dog. Immediately after she asked, "Why do you have green eyes and not black and brown like mine?" It was at that moment that I realized that these kids really did see me as different. When I first arrived to Korea I never really felt different from other people around me, even though I was in an unfamiliar environment. In the melting pot of the United States, I have always been exposed to many different cultures and races. After all, I grew up in Chicago and lived the better years of my life in Orange County California. I attributed my uneasiness in Korea to my unrecognizable surroundings. A few months after I first arrived to Korea, I took a closer look around and I began to see eyes staring at me; in the street, at the store, in the parking lot of the school. When I looked in the mirror I saw a tall, young, plain-looking woman. But many Korean women saw me (and still see me) as exotic, fair-skinned, and I'm bashful to say, beautiful. Of course, Korea is a homogenous society in which almost everyone possesses the same traits: thin, black hair, fair skin. This environment is very different than the mixture of people in my own country. In California, I'm just another face in the crowd. When you come to Korea, expect heads to turn your way when you're in public. It will be no big deal to you if you are capable of ignoring this kind of 'staring' behavior, or it may not even bother you at all. For me, it was a little bit difficult to adjust to in the beginning. Remember, Korean people don't often see foreigners, especially if they are in a small city or town. Korea has only been modernized for about sixty years, and within that time the country has recently started opening its doors more and more to global business, foreign labor, and immigration. The country is still trying to adjust to the changing society in which culture, habits, and people are changing. A good example of this is going to a simple department store. As a five-foot nine-inch woman, it has always been frustrating to try to buy a decent fitting bra or even a pair of shoes that fit. It has also been frustrating knowing that my last pair of ripped pantyhose would be exactly that—the last pair. Department stores do not keep up with the demand for larger sizes. Many modern Korean women are having the same 'shopping' problems I have always had, because modern Koreans are changing as well. They are taller, fuller, and require bigger shoe sizes. When I walk into a clothing or shoe section of a store, a clerk will often wave me away and say "no big size." I have reason to believe that because I am a foreigner they automatically assume that I will need an unusually large size. That's not always true. Sometimes I get lucky depending on the brand. I find that Korean women are sometimes surprised when they meet a petite foreigner (petite meaning smaller than they are). They expect foreigners, especially Westerners, to be bigger than the average Korean.

It's easy for a Westerner to feel self-conscious of his body when shopping or walking around in Korea, especially if he is very tall and his head hits the tops of doorways (and the holding pole on the ceiling of the bus). Of course you can expect some snickering if this happens. In my opinion, it's easy to lose self-esteem and good **body image** when you're larger or taller than everyone around you, and it becomes a chore to find your size. It's important to look past this and try and maintain a healthy body image, regardless. Of course, this is easier said than done. It's advantageous if you possess a strong personality with a ton of will power. It helps to shop in foreigner districts and chain department stores. Also, you will have less of a problem in the big cities, especially Seoul. Among a variety of different people of different sizes, as well as many foreigners and Westerners, you may feel more like you belong and that you're not sticking out in the crowd.

Even though many adults' perceptions of me were flattering, my students perceptions of me were not so flattering. Korean children are rarely exposed to foreigners outside of a hagwon classroom, so when they are, it becomes a bit jarring for them. At first, they will stare, gawk, and even cry if you get too close to them. Elementary and high school kids often glare, giggle, or sometimes just run away. A foreigner not accustomed to being perceived as 'different' can be easily confused when seeing this kind of behavior from children. What can start off as a morale booster can easily turn into a morale breaker in a relatively short amount of time. Being perceived of as 'different' was, by far, the most difficult thing to deal with during my time in Korea. After about six months, I developed a kind of suspicion that everywhere I went someone was looking at me or talking about me. It was a self-destructive suspicion that was difficult to snap out of. Many foreigners, however, are able to deal with this very well and humorously, and I suggest you do your best to do the same. It's important to remember that Korean children's staring stems from wonder and interest. If you are anything other than Asian in South Korea, there is no doubt you will encounter intrusively staring eyes (especially if you have blonde hair and light skin, or if you are of African descent). If you remember to take it as a simple cultural perception rather than an intrusion, it can help you cope with the situation better.

Korean communication is based on politeness and social hierarchy. Westerners will often address other Westerners casually depending on the surroundings, and will not pay too much attention to the social standing or age of the person they are addressing. This behavior seems strange to many Koreans, especially older Koreans. They will almost always use language that is appropriate to how old you are relative to them. If you are younger than the Korean who is speaking to you, he/she will use casual language without honorifics. If you are older than the Korean who is speaking to you, he/she will use more polite language full of honorifics. Because, you being a Westerner are not likely to adjust your body language or level of speech when speaking to a Korean, he/she may think you're brash or rude. This may be the first impression a Korean (especially an older Korean) may have of you. In my experience, middle-age and older Koreans think Westerners are sometimes rude, shameless, and too liberal in thought and action. Don't worry too much about this. Koreans whom I have become good friends with quickly realize this is just a stereotype. When my landlord found out that my boyfriend and I were living together and not married, he was quite surprised and he actually scoffed at me! But later on, he realized that we weren't such bad people. My advice is to be yourself and don't worry too much about conforming to the complex verbal and nonverbal communication structure of Korea. The people that matter the most will see and learn how you truly are, regardless of their original perceptions of Westerners.

Classroom Culture

The first school that I taught at was a bit of an elite and expensive English-speaking kindergarten and hagwon. The school was small, about four classrooms of ten children each, and boasted a global education program with an emphasis on the English language. Of course, there is not much 'teaching' and 'lecture' you can do with a bunch of five and six year olds, but the main purpose was to get them started on doing activities in English and speaking in English. It's a big deal for Korean parents to send their children to an English-speaking school. Parents believe that English is the global language needed for business and work, and the sooner they get their kids started with learning it, the more opportunities their kids will have when they get older (not to mention being able to get into a good university). Just by observing the amount of cram schools in the entire country, it's no secret that education, in general, is a big deal in Korea. I would even be so bold as to say that education is emphasized more in Korea than in the United States! Most children (and high school students) go to school all day, and after the day is done, go to school again, or sometimes learn from a private tutor that comes to the home. The entire day is filled with educational lectures and activities, leaving little room for play, T.V., or recreation. School can also be year-round, however, most schools have around a month of vacation between years. Korean high school students definitely don't get a job like many Western high school students do. In the United States, teenagers will babysit or get part-time jobs after school so that they can save some extra money to buy a car or other things. Many of my students in the States had jobs because they had to play a part in supporting their families. Basically, they worked to pull their weight in the household. This is unheard of in Korea. Korean students, rich, middle class, or poor, are encouraged by their families to spend their entire time studying. They are supported by their parents well throughout college and into adulthood. Mandatory military duty for Korean males postpones their job search, and it's not uncommon to find Koreans starting their first job when they are twenty-six years old!

Of course, I recognized first-hand how unproductive my Korean students became after going to school and studying non-stop for a twelve to thirteen-hour day. By the time the students came to my classroom, sometimes even at 5:00 or 6:00 in the evening, they were drained. This made it difficult for me to even teach, since students had no energy for activities and even put their head on their desks to nap. It is certainly a task to motivate over-worked students, especially if they know they have more classes after mine that may or may not last until midnight.

Kids can be funny creatures, and if you're teaching really little ones, the classroom culture can be quite a shock, especially for the first few days. Out of the ten five-year olds in my kindergarten class, one was so nervous her first day of school that she vomited all over her desk. The other kids, of course, thought it was funny and screamed the Korean equivalent to "Ewwwww!" Of course, every student leaped to touch the vomit, which was oozing over the edges of the desk. But after the brouhaha was over the girl continued to laugh and play just like nothing every happened. I wish I had that mentality; to forget my most embarrassing moments at the drop of a hat. Most of my kids had no shame. They lifted their skirts, pulled down their pants, scratched their behinds, and picked their noses in front of everybody in the room and thought absolutely nothing of it. At the time, I didn't know if this was normal or not. I had never worked with little kids before. However, that was so opposite of what I imagined Asian schoolchildren did. I had this picturesque image in my mind that each child would sit in their desk, with his hands folded in front of him, quiet, not uttering so much as a whisper. I was wrong. I thought *these aren't kids! They're devils in disguise!*

Depending on the age you teach, you can expect a lot of different levels, attitudes and emotions in the classroom. I taught kindergarten for the first half of the day (three to six-year-olds), which was more like daycare and babysitting in English, and elementary-age kids for the second half of the day, which was a more structured lecture. This included a lot of conversation and activity as well. The elementary kids were part of a hagwon program. As I mentioned before, hagwons are separate academies that serve to supplement children's' daily education, however, in the case of my school, it was a standard kindergarten and hagwon combined. I had kindergartners in the morning and elementary students in the afternoon. Although we received the books to get material from, we (the teachers) were responsible for developing, organizing, and teaching the material. There were no pre-set lesson plans. Expect to be in the same situation if working for a kindergarten or hagwon, as there are usually no specific standards that need to be met.

I can't say which group of students (kindergarten or elementary) was easier to teach. It depends on what age one is more compatible with. If you like a more structured English class, complete with lecture, discussion and homework, than the older, elementary-age, middle school, or high school students are the better bet. If you like to sit around with a bunch of five-year-olds and color, play and sing songs all day, then the kindergarteners may be more suitable for you. If you don't want to deal with behavior problems, and you like students who actually want to be in your classroom and will provide their undivided attention at all times (or if you just can't deal with children), then a university job, or an adult hagwon, is the best way to go. Adults pay a lot of money to attend academies; they're less likely to slack around. If you work in any classroom with children, expect there to be quiet students and rambunctious students. In my experience, if your Korean students don't understand very much English, they will tend to tune you out as soon as you speak to them. As a result, they'll get bored and begin to misbehave. This is standard behavior in the Korean English classroom. Once you find a happy balance with classroom management, and once your children start getting accustomed to your rules and methods of communication, they will calm down and listen more. Also, many disorders that we recognize in the West are not really taken into consideration when diagnosing a child's misbehavior or pace of learning. For example, I have had a lot of special needs children with syndromes and ADHD (Attention Deficit and Hyperactivity Disorder) in my Korean classrooms, and I have had a heck of a time controlling them. Other Korean parents and teachers would simply dismiss students' bad behavior as 'high energy' and blame learning disorders on the student just being 'disinterested in the topic'. Medications were not administered to students who, I believed, truly needed them, and as a result, the entire class would suffer whenever that 'special' child with 'high energy' would have a fit and throw every chair he could across the room. Of course, very severe misbehavior is rare, and other Korean teachers (and the principal) will most likely do everything they can to help you with classroom management. Just recognize that there are special needs children in Korean classrooms and you have to deal with them as-is, no medication and no special facilities. Take advantage of any help offered by other staff.

The university route is considered the Cadillac of all English teaching jobs in Korea. In many expatriates' opinions, it is the best route to take if you want maximum motivation in the classroom. As I mentioned before, you must be qualified to teach at a university with a minimum of master's degree. The classroom culture at universities, however, is very different than at children's schools. Both types of schools have their positives and negatives, but if you have the privilege to work with adults you'll find that most of them are very eager to learn English. They are more self-motivated and better-disciplined than children are. This makes the university classroom culture less behavior-driven and more productive. Instead of having to spend fifty percent of your time disciplining (as you do when teaching children), you'll be spending almost one-hundred percent of your time actually teaching material. Adults already know how to behave, so it maximizes your teaching and their learning. There are two things, however, that can become extremely frustrating for the Western English teacher to cope with and understand when working with university students. These two things are: lack of active response and lack of creative and independent thinking.

    The Korean education system has been a lot like an 'assembly line'. The teacher lectures and spits out tons of information while children take notes and absorb it. Then, the students are shuffled onto the next class and do the exact same routine all over again. Questions during lecture are certainly not encouraged. This would take time away from all the information the teacher must teach the students in a short period of time. Class and lecture times are focused on quantity, not quality. If you're wondering what happens if a student doesn't understand the material the teacher is spewing out, the usual answer is: nothing. If you are a Korean student, it is considered humiliating to admit that you don't understand something. If you do admit it, you run the risk of being regarded as stupid or slow. I have learned to expect in my classroom that when I ask students if they understand what I just taught, they will always answer "yes", even if they don't. Korean teachers will argue that that is what a hagwon is for, to study the material further and practice and repeat as much as you can so that when you come back to regular school the next morning, you can catch up. This lack of active participation and response (raising hands, asking questions, initiating discussion) is a serious annoyance to the Western English teacher in the Korean classroom. It doesn't take long for you to realize that Korean students just don't know how to 'come up with an idea' and 'discuss'. In the United States, the education system encourages students to respond aloud to questions, ask them often, and raise one's hand if something is not understood. American teachers also encourage their students to avoid humiliating snickering when someone doesn't understand. Students regard other students who are vocal in class as being 'smart' and 'outgoing'. In the Korean classroom, students regard other students who are vocal in class as being 'arrogant' and 'noncompliant', disrupting the harmony and flow of the class. So, you can see why the lack of active response can be jarring to the first-time English teacher who is accustomed to the behavior of Western children.

Some of these cultural factors, such as the 'assembly line' education focusing on quantity not quality, may be an influence in the lack of creative thinking. As children, Korean students don't have many opportunities in classes to do group activities, debates, speeches, and creative projects. Doing these things would take time away from lecture and note-taking. So, when these students enter a Western university in the United States, Canada, or Australia, they don't do very well. As a matter of fact, many of them fail miserably, unless they are taking classes that require them to methodically memorize and robotically perform a routine. Otherwise, in a Western university classroom, they are expected to have independent ideas and do presentations in which discussion may be involved. These tasks don't come easy to Korean students.

Luckily, the current Korean government is trying to change the education system that has been prominent in Korea for so long. They are beginning to finally realize that this type of education has become outdated and is no longer an effective vehicle for producing globally competitive Korean citizens. I have had the opportunity to teach adult company employees and there is nothing worse than sitting in a room full of thirty to fifty-year-olds with decent English speaking ability who are afraid to ask you a question. Worse yet, they can't even invent a simple story and write it on paper. It was alarming to me, and it required a lot of planning and effort to be able to change these students' learning habits. When I initiated a group project or hands-on activity in my elementary classroom, students would just scatter around, having no idea what to do or how to communicate and organize their ideas. The fact that girls refused to work with the boys made things even more difficult! They wouldn't even look at each other! Overall, when you teach in a Korean classroom, the students will expect you to tell them how to think and what to write. Don't succumb to this method of teaching. It may take six months or so, but their habits can be changed—at least during the short while they're in your classroom.

Besides the government initiating change, there are educational programs and schools in Korea that are also trying to reverse the 'assembly line' education philosophy. My other half works for a graduate school for Korean English teachers. These teachers attend this school to update their certification and master their English skills. He is encouraged to teach these teachers creative and effective teaching habits as well as thinking skills that they can use in their own classrooms. The graduate school's goal is to reverse this Korean trend of memorizing and spitting out, and produce students and young adults who can critically think for themselves, be creative, and not be afraid to communicate in English. It starts with teaching the teachers. If the Korean teachers change their teaching approach, it can become groundbreaking for their students.

What Kind of Behavior to Expect

Restrictions and rules concerning classroom management and behavior vary in children's schools and hagwons. Corporal punishment is present in just about any school, however, usually only Korean teachers are allowed to administer this type of punishment. I have never met a Western teacher who felt comfortable with striking a student. Students are spanked, hit on their heads and hands with large wooden spoons, and forced to hold chairs above their heads until their arms become fatigued. This can seem like rough punishment to the Western teacher. In my time in Korea, I have hardly seen a behavior that can't be taken care of with alternative solutions, avoiding corporal punishment altogether. But until the Korean educational system finally transforms from a traditional to a Western-style system, corporal punishment will be a fact of life. All teachers in children's schools are allowed to touch students. Young children are picked up, thrown around, and showered with kisses. In my experience working with very young children (age four), I see girls and boys playing together without real regard to gender differences. It's not until they get older, elementary age, that they begin to segregate themselves and form gender-based friendships and alliances. As I mentioned before, most of my students who refused to work or play with a member of the opposite sex, did so until age nine to eleven. When they reached age nine to eleven, they seemed to care less about gender differences and age. After eleven, the discrimination was apparent once again.

As early as kindergarten, students are not held back or protected from much in the classroom. Children (four year-olds) are given scissors and sharp objects without a second thought. This is unheard of at most kindergartens in the United States. It's all a very flexible 'live and learn' kind of attitude, which has its positives and negatives. On a school camping trip I went on with the last hagwon I worked for, the children were leaving their cabins to go to the corner store, buy fireworks, and shoot them off in the middle of the night. These children, ages eight to thirteen, had no supervision when purchasing the fireworks and were even given lighters by the store owner to ignite the fireworks with. When I finally caught them doing this, I paid a visit to the cabin of the principal and the head teacher. I thought it would be better to tell them since many of the younger children didn't speak English and wouldn't understand if I told them to stop. When I told the principal and the head teacher that the children were igniting fireworks by the back road, they didn't give much thought to it. The head teacher stated, "So? That's okay. They know what they're doing. Anyways, if we tell them not to do it, they'll still do it anyways." I was utterly surprised at the response I got! The reality finally sunk in. It was certainly a live and learn situation. All I could think about was one of our students going home the next day with a missing finger. However, nobody seemed to be worried about them. In the United States, the opposite would have happened. Teachers would have had to confiscate the fireworks and possibly discipline the children and call their parents the next day. Anyways, I'm pretty sure American children wouldn't be able to purchase the fireworks without a parent present in the first place. This is an enormous cultural difference to take note of.

Children in Korean kindergartens seem to have license to go wild, and the teacher is often expected to put up with it and accept it. The teacher can conduct class with a lot of freedom. He has room to develop curriculum according to his own teaching style and can use his own methods of punishment. Korean parents spoil their children and want to know that their children are being spoiled at school. There is almost never a parent-teacher conference unless absolutely necessary, for example, if a child misbehaves unmanageably more than a dozen times. Western kindergarten teachers are accustomed to reacting negatively to misbehavior, and punishing or disciplining children by not letting them participate in certain fun activities as well as taking away privileges. However, in my experience with Korean kindergartens, children's privileges and allowances are rarely taken away, even if a child's behavior is out of control. Kindergarten children are ever so spoiled in this way. So, in many ways, Western teachers are given conflicting advice: 'Your classroom is *your* classroom, and you're free to manage and discipline any way you see fit, however, try not to take away any privileges when children misbehave—and by all means, don't say anything bad on their progress reports!'

There is also the problem of teaching Korean children to accept defeat. Making them understand that there is always a winner and a loser when playing games seems impossible. In Korea, children are conditioned to believe that being first place is the one and only option. There is no second place and certainly no third place. There are no *'I did my best!'* excuses. I have never seen so many children cry and throw active fits when they don't win or come out on top. Parents push and push their children to be the best, even when it is beyond their capacity. This was recently demonstrated at an English contest in Seoul that my other half was a judge for. He had to judge about thirty children performing English speeches on various topics. Of course, there were winners in the end, and it didn't surprise him to see so many children crying when they didn't win first place. Parents carried on that, by God, it should have been *their* children that won. This kind of behavior is also very present in the children's schools. I remember parents calling my school and arguing with the Korean teachers that their child should be in a more advanced class, even though we knew that the advanced class was beyond the child's capacity. Sometimes we would have to honor the parents' request just to maintain peace and harmony, and to 'play along' with a certain social hang-up the parent had. For example, there was a mother who was trying to 'keep up with the Jones's by putting her child in the advanced class because her neighbor's child happened to be in the advanced class. The parent would have been embarrassed and could have 'lost face' if her child wasn't at the same English level as her neighbor's child. Of course, because of this social competition, the children always suffer and are put in a situation they just can't handle. In the end, the class material becomes overwhelming and the child ends up failing, placing an even bigger burden on the parents. I know that there are times when this happens in Western schools as well. However, in Western schools, children are conditioned to believe that any special needs will be attended to, and being number two or number three (or even number eight) is not cause for embarrassment as long as you did your best. Western schools are equal opportunity, but parents and teachers recognize that their children have their strong points and weak points. The weak points must be accepted and worked on.

I believe that it is important to add that young Korean children are extremely coddled and fussed over by their parents and their Korean teachers. This affects their behavior in a colossal way. I have witnessed this leading to major discipline problems. This coddling behavior stems from the fact that the birth rate in Korea is low, and many couples nowadays only have one or two children. The cost of living for the typical middle-class Korean family is high, and with the mother often working as a stay-at-home mom, it is difficult to financially care for more children than that. Therefore, the few children that couples do have are spoiled to the extreme, and they expect that everyone in their children's lives spoil them as well. Seeing children get coddled, especially after they have misbehaved, was extremely tough for me to get used to. I came from a teaching environment where teachers are not supposed to touch the children under any circumstances unless a life was in danger or a child needed to be restrained. Seeing kindergarten children kissed, hugged, bounced on knees, and thrown up in the air was an enormous shock to me. Korean parents expect Western teachers to 'roll with the punches' and simply deal with their children's behavior problems, after all, that's what the teacher is getting paid for. Discipline problems range from throwing active fits, to screaming, to excessive crying, to constant attention seeking. Many of my youngest children could not complete their own work unless I was standing right beside them giving them much praise along the way. They were extremely dependent and required constant attention—more than any American student I have ever had. This became a problem when I had up to fifteen students at a time. I couldn't stand next to every student and give them constant hugs, kisses, and praise like they expected. I relied on students who were more independent to set an example for the rest of the students. I often wondered how these children can go from being so dependent on praise and help, to being able to purchase fireworks and shoot them off without anyone by their side to cheer on. It had become quite a mystery to me.

Nevertheless, many Western teachers that I have seen don't stand for the excessive coddling and misbehavior in their classrooms. I have seen Western teachers set very strict rules, policies, and reward systems that, even though they took Korean parents and staff by surprise, worked as an excellent system in keeping order and sanity. Many inexperienced teachers don't know how to deal with this double standard of being given complete control, yet being told how to conduct their classroom, and as a result, stop caring. At this point, it would be important for the Western teacher to get a clear set of guidelines on how the principal expects the classroom to be conducted.

I had one student, an eight-year-old boy named Kwan-Hoon, who was a rollercoaster of emotion and attitude. I taught him privately at his home during my second teaching job as a mobile teacher. What an experience that was! Kwan-Hoon was one of those children that ordered his mother around and whined a lot while I was there in order to show off in front of the teacher. He never wanted to learn any of the lessons I prepared or do the activities in which I thought he would like. He was a fairly advanced English speaker who, due to his father's job, had lived a few years in Philadelphia. Every class period became more of a nightmare because of his difficult attitude and mood swings. Also, his inability to deal with loss when playing games caused him to throw objects around the room in a fit of rage. His mother, being the patient woman that she was, coddled him in return. I couldn't stand seeing her do this. This was one of the most misbehaved children I had ever seen, and I seriously thought about quitting the class simply because I couldn't come up with any material that was pleasing enough for him. Finally, one day, the volcano erupted. Kwan-Hoon would often cheat to ensure he would win during a game. That particular day we played Junior Scrabble, and I made him promise to play honestly and not cheat. Of course, he promised. I wanted to test him. But as soon as I started winning, his temptation got the best of him. He started to cheat. After several times of reminding him about his promise, he still couldn't stop. So, I calmly announced that since he was cheating, I would begin cheating as well. Luckily, I was the better cheater. After ten minutes of watching me cheat and watching me win, he just couldn't take it anymore. The entire board game and every piece on it went flying into the air. Everything was on the floor, and there was Kwan-Hoon, crying and screaming and throwing a fit. I admit, I probably should have prevented myself from winning just to keep the peace. After all, the game was about learning English vocabulary. But when I saw this boy behave this way, I was in shock. I truly didn't know what to do. I just sat there and stared, and after ten minutes of watching Kwan-Hoon throw a fit, I stood up and left. Of course, as I was walking out the door, his mother apologized profusely for her son's irrational behavior, but I could only imagine how much she coddled him after I had left. I was positive she reassured him that it was all going to be okay and that he was sure to win at the next game. This was yet another example of a child not being able to cope with loss and second place. His behavior spoiled every lesson we had.

Unfortunately, Kwan-Hoon's behavior is very representative of the behavior of many Korean children. It doesn't help that the Western teacher is often less respected than the Korean teacher. Very young children often see Western teachers as a source of brief companionship and entertainment for one or two hours per week, which is not enough time to develop the trust and respect the Western teacher deserves. Kwan-Hoon wouldn't have behaved as bad as he did if I were his Korean homeroom teacher. I know this because I witnessed the change of children's behavior everyday according to which teacher was in their classroom. Of course, there are other factors that play into how much (or how less) students respect their Western English teachers, one important factor being their level of English. When children don't understand what is being said to them, obviously, they don't understand what is expected of them. This communication difficulty is frustrating when an English teacher scolds them. Many times, very young children just don't understand that they're being scolded. During my work as a mobile English teacher, I was considered by my students as that 'weekly visiting foreign friend' who would stick around for an hour, dance around, and teach them songs. Of course, my adult students always took me a lot more seriously and treated me with utter respect. But the children were a different story. My weekly visitations with the children, whether privately or at a school, were hardly enough time for them to learn and remember my boundaries and expectations. This worked against me a great deal in that I could not fulfill my objective in teaching them English (or at least, in teaching them as much English as I wanted them to learn). I was too busy trying to get their attention and cure behavior problems. I eventually gained respect from my students at the kindergarten in Cheonan City, however, I was with those children for most of the day. They had plenty of time to learn and understand my boundaries and expectations. The initial problem was not being able to understand my English and my communication patterns. Once the students and I got over this stressful 'hump', the days became smoother. Nevertheless, it was incredibly difficult to establish my presence in the classroom as an individual to be respected. If you're planning on working with young and/or kindergarten-age children, it's a good idea to keep a strong head, a strong set of boundaries, and a lot of patience. If you can do this, the experience can be rewarding.

The Westerner's Perspective of His Job

Earlier I talked briefly about the lack of respect and behavioral problems Western English teachers sometimes encounter in their kindergarten and hagwon classrooms. I offered my theoretical explanation for this as being mainly a cultural and communication barrier. The students see the Western teacher as the 'visiting English friend' who babbles at them in an unintelligible language and whose physical appearance and mannerisms may be different and quite humorous to them. Basically, these perceptions of the Western teacher by the students (and vice versa) stem from the inability of both sides to effectively communicate and a simple lack of experience with the other individual's culture. This inexperience and inability to communicate not only exists between the Western teacher and his students, but also exists between the Western teacher and his fellow Korean staff. This issue of communication seriously needs to be considered by both the Korean and the Western staff. Cultural barriers that develop as a result of ineffective communication can result in negative perceptions of the job and the people. By not understanding, Korean staff can develop bad perceptions of the Western staff and vice versa. The individual I talk about in the following paragraph had developed a lot of frustration and negativity throughout his time working in Korea.

At the first school I taught at, the combination kindergarten and hagwon, I had a co-worker named Rob whom I became very close friends with. He was one of the first people who I can say was part of my support system of friends. Rob was from San Francisco and he came to Korea to teach because he was in a similar situation I was in. He was caught in a job slump and was unable to find work during my country's economical and political circus. Rob proved to be the most interesting character I had ever met and a wonderful friend who boldly said many things I wouldn't have dared say while present in a foreign country. He provided a lot of comic relief, especially during my most stressful times.

    Rob's experience in Korea had not been a very good one. As a matter of fact, it was downright appalling for him at times. Rob's personality was really 'tell-it-like-it-is', and he used the enhanced version of this character inside his classroom. The children in his class were only about six or seven years old, and it was always uncertain how far we could go with humor since we were teaching in a conservative culture. Rob was reprimanded one time for writing in a student's progress report that he (the student) had a behavior problem, and that he "would have a great future in a Korean prison." Of course, the student's parents were not too happy about this comment. As a matter of fact, they were furious, and the director of the school (our boss) quickly reminded Rob that the school was still a business and the object was to get the parents to keep their kids enrolled, not to scare them away. The director asked Rob, in the utmost, polite Korean way, to apologize to the student and his parents, and indeed, Rob did. Everyone moved on. However, a bit of friction developed between Rob and the director. Later, at one point, Rob made the decision to involve the children in his political viewpoints. This wasn't as serious as the previous offense, but it was very funny. These children were beginners in the English language, just barely learning words like 'cat', and 'dog', and 'bathroom', and there was Rob, teaching them how to chant "Bush no good! Bush no good!" (Referring to the American President George W. Bush). Of course, the children had no idea what was being taught to them and what they were chanting. Children in Korean classrooms are taught to just repeat. Don't ask questions, just repeat what is said. This is what made it so comical!

Because of Rob's outgoing personality, independent character, and fearless ability to ask questions and question authority, Korean staff (and some Western staff who had been teaching in Korea for awhile) found it a bit difficult to get along with him. Communication with Korean staff, especially the director, was often poor and misunderstood. Rob also did exactly the opposite of what the bosses wanted him to do; he distanced himself from the 'group' and stayed a loner. A loner was just who he was. This anti-team attempt went against the harmony and collectivist nature of the school culture. He didn't participate in staff activities and never involved himself in karaoke and Friday night drinking bouts with bosses. This sincerely pissed off Korean staff. The director viewed this behavior as unreasonable and antisocial, and assumed Rob was deliberately trying to make waves in the workplace. In fact, Rob was not trying to do this. This was just the type of character he had. This misunderstanding of characters, and Rob's resentment of what the Korean staff's expectations of him were, created a whirlwind of conflict and miscommunication.

Overall, even though Rob was a very non-conventional English teacher, he never had any ill-intentions for the children he taught. In fact, he was a dedicated, hard-working teacher that cared for his children a great deal. His comical outbursts and wacky demeanor were meant to make stressful situations light, to make the children laugh, and to take the tension out of what was becoming an incredibly tense atmosphere to work in. As time went on and the communication gap between the Korean and Western staff became greater and greater, Rob was always there to break the ice and 'sitcom-ize' the situation. Nevertheless, he always took his job seriously. Rob was the type of friend that was so valuable to have around.

Poor communication and misunderstandings caused Rob to become dissatisfied with Korea and his job. His perception of work and the people around him was corrupted by simple miscommunication.

The Impact of Support on the Ability to Adjust

Rob failed to culturally adapt in so many ways. Rob's new environment was so new and strange to him in comparison to his native environment (San Francisco), he just didn't know how to deal with it. These things affected his ability to develop friendships with Korean people. He distanced himself from everyone around him and made sure that everyone understood he was a loner. In turn, the lack of friends had negatively impacted his cultural adjustment. He felt like he had no support, until he occasionally started allowing himself to develop a friendship with me and another English teacher.

Rob avoided Korea the best that he could while living in Korea. He didn't eat most Korean foods and avoided learning the Korean language (except for a few words like 'hello', 'thank you', and 'goodbye'). When Rob began his teaching position at the school, the school had just opened and he was one of the first teachers. Because there wasn't a foreign/Western staff already established, Rob did not immediately have a proper support system available to him. He walked to work alone, ate lunch alone, and barely ever left his apartment. It wasn't long, however, that the rest of the Western staff became hired. It was at that time that he had the chance to lean on them as much as he could. I believe that if he would have immediately established friendships and a support system, his transition into his new environment and new job would have been smoother and less confusing. Not being able to make friends right away affected Rob's attitude, this in turn, affected his experience and ability to adjust. The result was a long, tough year of fulfilling a contract. When I and another new teacher, Jane, came to the school a few months later, Rob's tension was noticeably eased, even though some damage had already been done.

If I learned anything from Rob, he taught me the utter importance of establishing a support system. He taught me that if you resist making friends, you fail to culturally adapt, and your experience abroad may be a tough one to get through. While working with Rob, little did he know that he and Jane served as *my* only support systems. Jane became an exceptional support system because she spent so much time showing me the ropes and teaching me to become fearless of my environment. Rob was a good support system because he was my 'sympathetic' buddy and my shoulder to cry on.

It's best to maintain friendships with other people who are in the same situation as you for several reasons: first, friends provide the emotional support you need to survive in a foreign environment such as a country you've never been to before. Second, they most likely already know the ins and outs of communicating with the locals if they have arrived before you (including being able to speak some Korean). Your new friends can teach you how to verbally communicate in situations that call for it, such as introducing yourself to others, taking a taxi, finding a bathroom, or even just expressing what you want or need to your boss (who may or may not speak English). Third, establishing friendships makes you feel like you're not alone and gives you the confidence to tackle any situation you encounter, whether it be cultural or communicative. You're more likely to go out and explore your surroundings if you are encouraged to do so by your friends, or if you simply have someone to go with. Overall, the Western staff you work with may run into the same cultural barriers and communication difficulties that you may run into, and if you stick together, you can get through any negative or confusing experiences together. Whether or not you have a support system can greatly impact your experience living and working in South Korea.

My recommendation is to seek a teaching position at a school where there are other Western teachers. It is important to share the current experience together, regardless of how long those teachers have been in Korea. Once you begin working, use them as your support system. I have had the experience of being the only Western teacher at a school, and it was an extremely lonely experience. Of course, the Korean staff understood only a little about what I was going through, but because I was a foreigner, they tended to leave me out of conversations, meetings, and group decisions. Of course, that was never a good move. It only created more misunderstanding and negative energy. I really had to actively include myself in group happenings and not wait to be invited. At times, my lonely situation did affect my ability to adjust. To resolve the issue, I would quickly call a friend or family member, and my perspective would spin right back to normal.

Chapter 6:
Communicating With Korean Co-Workers

I found the following comment excerpts on a free listing and comments exchange board (called the expat soapbox) on the online version of the Korea Herald Newspaper. In the first comment, it seems clear why the expatriate became frustrated. He talks about communication problems and the "wall of silence" between employer and employee. A logical response to the comment follows.

> 'I was wondering if I could share some opinions with you. Since coming to East Asia I have often found that there are problems working here because of the constant "wall of silence" which can surround the foreigner, and which leads to friction because of lack of understanding. What prompted me to write was my being called into the Boss's office yesterday because it seems that my badly-behaved kids are getting angry with me getting angry with them. So I am getting lectured because they are lazy, bored and misbehaving. But my immediate thoughts after wards were: "Well, shouldn't they have told me about this a long time ago? And why has this started just now?" You see, in my experience, teacher meetings in East Asia always exclude the foreigners. I was told (while I was in Taiwan) that this is so the foreigner does not "lose face", but the effect of this is that if there are any serious developments, the foreigner is always the last to know. Nowadays, in the West, we are accustomed to the notion that the flow of information within a business is paramount, but here this notion

> is flouted and this "incommunicability" compounds the foreigner's problems. Yet the same people are paying you good money to be as useful for them as possible - or so one would suppose. And as you might expect, I become ever more frustrated. I want to do the job they want me to do - but they never discuss it until a problem has already transformed itself into a crisis, and there is little that can be done about it. I want to avoid such situations because they are bad for a private institution, but I can't help thinking that they make their own problems. Any thoughts, anyone?'-"Andrew"

This teacher mentions a phenomenon that was all-too-familiar to me during my teaching days in Korea; the exclusion of Western staff at teachers' meetings. This exclusion proved to have dire consequences in that Western teachers were never informed until the very last moment of crucial changes in policy, calendar activities, days off, and information regarding the children. In the situation of my first school, the Korean director only excluded Western staff because he was unable to express the contents of the meeting appropriately in English. Therefore, he was afraid of not communicating effectively what he needed to communicate to the Western staff. It was much easier for him to be thorough and precise with the Korean staff. Of course, it was a mistake for him to think that the Korean staff would then relay his messages to the Western staff, because they never did. They couldn't because they were too shy to speak the little bit of English they knew. Really, this was a no-win situation. In my opinion, the best thing for the director to do was to hold two separate meetings, one with the Korean staff and one with the Western staff, and to express himself the best that he could to the Western staff.

The following comment is a response to Andrew's comment found on the same exchange board.

> 'I don't want to sound harsh, but maybe the employer expected you to have known everything necessary to make those badly behaved kids in your class in your control. I know it would have been much easier if your boss had discussed everything with you from the beginning, but from the perspective of being a boss, your boss probably didn't want to spend time on teaching you about how to solve the problem, which is not unreasonable. He may have thought that you are hired because you are expected to know enough how to deal with those kids. Or the boss may have wanted to wait until the last moment so that you could sort out the problem on your own with due respect to your being their teacher, which is not unusual in the Korean way of dealing with employees. I know it may not be fair to you in Western perspective, but hey...there is no easy life once you leave your home. '-"Cindy"

Teaching in the Land of Kimchi

One day I had a conversation with a thirty-four-year-old English teacher from Canada, Glen, who was living in Seoul for two and a half years. To sum up the conversation, he felt exactly the way Andrew felt in regards to communication difficulties: frustrated and perhaps just fed up. Glen had said that his first year in Korea was great—very exhilarating. He was in a new culture and felt like he was fulfilling his adventurous character. But by the second year, everything was predictable. It became a struggle to interact with the Korean people, and he claimed that it seemed like every Korean person he communicated with seemed to take his comments and expressions out of context. This was very likely, and I don't doubt Glen's claim. I never invalidated his feelings about Korean culture. However, I did take notice of his character, and perhaps it may have had something to do with the type of experiences he was having in Korea. In my experience communicating with Glen, I saw that he was a difficult person to communicate with. He would often interrupt me and dismiss my point of view. His personality may have had something to do with how his behavior and attitude developed as well. Glen also seemed to be very opinionated. He didn't hesitate to dish out what he was really thinking— even if it was not very pleasant. Overall, Glen's communicative inflexibility may have been the culprit of his communication problems.

A few days after I had received the job offer for teaching English in Daejon (my second contract), I had given my Korean director a one month notice and immediately began to pack. I was excited about the new job because I knew I would be working mostly one-on-one with students. At the time, I was massively frustrated with dealing with the bureaucracy of the kindergarten and the stress of communicating with very young children. I knew it was time for me to try something new. The very last day of work at the kindergarten my director bid me a heartfelt farewell (even though he somewhat held a grudge against me for leaving his school). But something he said, and the emotion he said it with, struck me as particularly interesting. As my director shook my hand, he told me that wherever I went and whatever I did, he hoped that Korea and its people had left a good impression on me. He said that whatever I thought about his school, he hoped that my experience in Korea will continue to be a good one. And as he said this, tears rolled down his face. At that final moment, I didn't know how to react. What was I supposed to say? All I could do was listen and think, expressionless. I thanked him, said goodbye, and went on my merry way. Back home in the U.S.A. I had never seen an employer react this way to an employee leaving—absolutely never!

Korean people are very concerned about how foreigners view their country and its people. I have seen looks of surprise on Korean people's faces when a foreigner expresses any kind of dissatisfaction about Korea—its food, its music, its way of life. Korean people are sensitive to comments like these, and there are many Koreans who have gone out of their way to make foreigners happy. At the same time, there are many foreigners and Western teachers who are disappointed in the way they have been treated by their employers and fellow Korean co-workers, and some have even take their aggression out mistakenly on the entire country and everyone around them. Even though Korean employers and co-workers often try to accommodate their foreign English teachers, it can be difficult for the foreigner to trust their intentions as being sincere because he cannot communicate and understand them in the way he is accustomed to. Unfortunately, on the part of the Western teacher, suspicion can develop against the Korean staff.

I believe that Koreans wanting so dearly for Westerners to maintain a good impression of them had become a problem for me when I communicated with fellow Korean co-workers. It became a problem in many situations. The Korean teachers during my first contract were so worried about being polite and courteous when speaking to me, they answered questions positively even if they didn't really know the answers to the questions (or didn't really understand what I said). They were so afraid to say 'no', fearing it would be too rude. There was one teacher in particular, whom I could ask anything at all, and she would always just smile and answer "yeah, yeah, yeah." I called it the 'infamous yeah, yeah, yeah' response. Most of the time, she didn't understand what I was saying, but just to be compliant and polite, she answered "yeah, yeah, yeah" and hoped that she was answering correctly. She was too embarrassed to let me (or any of the other foreign staff) know when she didn't clearly understand. The "yeah, yeah, yeah's," got her in more hot water with the Western staff than what it was worth, and the foreign staff deemed her as unreliable. Take note of the following examples of a typical exchange with a Korean co-worker:

Question: "*Amy, are you staying late today?*" *Answer:* "*Yeah, yeah, yeah.*" *And then she goes home early.*

Question: "*Amy, can you take over and watch my class for a few minutes?*" *Answer:* "*Yeah, yeah, yeah, sure.*" *And then she's nowhere to be found.*

Question: "*Boss, is my class at 9:00 am tomorrow?*" *Answer:* "*Yeah, yeah, yeah,*" *And the next day I am late to my class which started at 8:30.*

Question: "*Boss, why did you confirm that my class was at 9:00 when it was really at 8:30?*" *Answer:* "*Oh, I'm sorry!!! I didn't hear you ask about that.*"

I had gotten in the habit of repeating questions and statements several times until I was absolutely sure that the person understood one hundred percent what I was saying. I would have rather had a person answer my question negatively and be honest, rather than smile and say 'yes' just to be compliant.

It's important to remember that Korean staff is extremely valuable when working at a school, especially when they are bilingual. They communicate concerns and act as a go-between for the foreign staff and the Korean director. They translate lessons, ideas, and activities to students that the Western teacher has difficulty explaining. They always take care of the odds and ends of organization—keeping classroom materials in check and up to date, maintaining discipline, and sometimes even decorating classrooms according to theme and season. Without a Korean staff, a Western teacher's job can become unmanageable and overwhelming. With this said, it is absolutely crucial to communicate openly and effectively, and keep a positive relationship with your Korean co-workers. A few simple "yeah, yeah, yeah's" can get the Western and Korean staff off to a bad start, and that can become a monster if you have an entire school year ahead of you. I simply propose that the best way to avoid any staff conflict and communication difficulties is to have a meeting at the beginning of the school year and once anyone new is hired. Discussion should include what the duties of the Korean staff are as well as the duties of the Western teaching staff, and what is expected of everyone. Ice-breakers and get-to-know-each-other activities can be included in the meeting. Unfortunately, this kind of meeting was never held in most of the places I had worked at, and from speaking to other foreign English teachers, I understand that this does not happen very often. As a result of culture clashes and communication problems between foreign and Korean staff, I have seen a kind of segregation developed in the school. I have seen situations where Western staff sticks together like glue, alienating themselves. I have also seen Korean staff trying desperately not to deal with Western staff. I believe if staff meetings that included everyone were held at my schools more often, the communication gap between foreign and Korean staff would have gotten narrower or perhaps closed altogether. The courtesy complex (always answering positively to avoid being rude) really created a communication gap in most of the schools I worked at, as it does in many other schools. Like I stated earlier, it's always important to repeat questions and statements more than once to ensure that the other person understands completely. Be patient and encourage the other person to listen very carefully and to not be so afraid of speaking English. It's also a good idea that Western staff encourages the Korean staff to repeat and clarify questions and statements more than once. Western staff should get in the habit of doing the same. This way, there is less doubt as to what is being asked and what is to be done. Verbal repetition and staff meetings are the solution to a harmonious relationship between Western and Korean staff.

Lost in Translation

It is without doubt that when one is living or traveling in another country, miscommunication at one point or another is inevitable. Things can get lost in translation and it can become a confusing, embarrassing, or comical episode. During my time in South Korea, there were many communication episodes that reminded me how my own culture had shaped my perception of things, including my way of understanding things. When I was young, I had taken language differences for granted, failing to recognize that culture shapes language and language shapes culture. I also failed to recognize that all nonverbal communication is not universal. There was a time in my life when I assumed that everything—every facial expression, body language, and verbal gesture—was to be understood in generally the same way universally. It wasn't until my anthropological studies in graduate school and my travel pursuits that I began to realize that this was an enormous fallacy. For example, American culture has taught us that a person smiling indicates that he is feeling happy or pleased. However, in some Asian cultures, a smile can indicate a person is uneasy, nervous, or even stressed. There is not just one way to interpret a smile. The same goes for verbal language. The meaning of one spoken statement can vary depending on who is speaking it and what culture they come from. For example, the translation of the word 'why' in Korean is 'whey', but it is not often used as a 'why' question. The word 'whey' is used as a 'what' question. So, if a friend calls you on your cell phone, it would be normal for an English speaker to answer "What do you want?" But if a Korean speaker answers the phone, he would say "Why?"

About two years ago I had the enlightening opportunity to visit Tokyo, Japan with two very close friends of mine. One of them was originally from Tokyo and the other was originally from Latin America. The three of us had been studying anthropology at the same university when we decided to take the trip together. Needless to say, I was a fairly tall, broad-shouldered Western female and my friend was a very tall, well-built Nicaraguan. The two of us stuck out like sore thumbs on the streets of Japan. This is a society in which the people are significantly shorter than Westerners. People would often gaze at us with a kind of awe, especially on the subway where you can see the reflections in the windows of people's staring faces. The whole thing was quite comical. I kept reminding myself not to let it ruin my self-image. One day, while a restaurant owner was trying to make room in the corner of his restaurant for us, he took a moment to stare up at us and then humorously referred to us as being very "nutritious" people. This was an interesting way to describe someone. Of course, we didn't protest his statement, and luckily, I understood the comment exactly the way I thought he meant it: we were large, healthy-looking foreigners who probably did not have any problems with our nutrition intake. This was a comment that could have been easily taken as an insult. 'Nutritious' could have been understood as 'fat'. Well, we took it with stride. But there are times when comments, or a particular look, are not understood by the receiver like it's meant, and a good-natured conversation can turn sour.

Comments like the one said to my Nicaraguan friend and I were plentiful during my stay in Korea as well. Some of them I understood and some of them I didn't. Early on in my first teaching contract, I belonged to a salsa-dancing club that was kind enough to accept a few Westerners as members. One night, the club had a salsa retreat in which we all sat around a fiery barbecue grill cooking, socializing, and occasionally dancing. There was a Korean man who sat beside me, and after a few moments of taking a good, solid look at me and the other foreigners, he said to me in broken English, "Melissa, you are very, very healthy." Of course, I remembered the 'nutritious' comment I received at the restaurant in Tokyo, so I thought I understood exactly what he meant—that I was 'nutritious'. After all, it was obvious that I was a lot bigger and taller than most of the Korean men and women in the group. So, I responded, "yes, yes, I know." At that moment, all the people roared with laughter as if I had said the funniest thing. Why were they laughing? For fifteen minutes I kept thinking why it was so funny for me to acknowledge my size. Then, one of the members whose English was more advanced recognized that something definitely got lost in translation. He explained to me that sometimes in Korean, the word 'healthy' is interchangeable with 'beautiful' and can mean the same thing. So, what the man meant to say to me was, "Melissa, you are very beautiful." But for me, the embarrassment was the "Yes, yes, I know" comment I made immediately after his statement. Everyone laughed when I said this because they perceived my response as being arrogant. Of course, later, everyone understood the reason behind the communication mishap. After that incident I had never again heard a Korean person substitute the word 'healthy' for 'beautiful'.

In general, Koreans use a lot of English vocabulary differently than what native English speakers are used to. Some English words are interpreted differently in Korean. The only advice I can give for native English speakers to avoid insult or miscommunication is to clarify all conversations and questionable comments, even if it means repeating or rephrasing things. Take the person's intentions into consideration. In many cultures, it is not rude to bluntly tell someone that he is fat. So, think before making an aggressive comeback to a Korean who is trying to tell you something the best way that he can in English. Also, Koreans that do speak English almost always have very different pronunciation. This results in many translation losses as well. Or course, foreigners that speak Korean cannot pronounce well either, so the misunderstanding can go both ways. In my experience, what makes it more difficult is that Koreans do not expect Westerners to actually speak Korean to them, so they're not actively listening for it, missing the sentence entirely and looking at the Westerner as if he just said something, well, foreign. This can happen even if the Westerner's Korean pronunciation is very good. The Korean individual missing what has been said by the Westerner results in the Westerner repeating the sentence two or more times before the Korean individual realizes that he is hearing Korean. This can be extremely frustrating, leaving the Westerner little confidence to speak because of fear of getting it wrong or not being understood. On the same note, it is often difficult for native English speakers to understand Koreans speaking English. Pronunciation is the key problem when Koreans learn English. Some Koreans learn English on a conversational level when they are young (elementary age), and most of their English education is limited to reading and writing only. So, their pronunciation is average to satisfactory. Overall, they are generally understood by native English speakers.

Because of the emphasis on reading and writing when learning English, Korean students lack opportunities to practice their listening comprehension and speaking skills. It is common to meet Koreans who have been learning English their entire lives and cannot speak a word of English, or cannot even understand when English is spoken to them. This is a problem that the Korean education system is trying to fix by requiring more speaking in the English classroom. I mentioned earlier in the book that Korean students do not often do debates, speeches, or group activities in the classroom, limiting their creative and conversational capabilities. Well, the Korean government is encouraging these types of activities at English hagwons and in English language classrooms. Hopefully, we will see more Korean students able to speak English and listen more effectively in the near future, making the Western teacher's job easier!

Once, I spent an entire private class period teaching a man how to properly pronounce the words 'girl' and 'world'. This was a problem for him because of the 'r' and the 'l' being right beside each other. One of the biggest problems when Koreans speak English is switching their 'r's and 'l's. If there is an 'r' toward the beginning of the word, a native Korean speaker will pronounce it as an 'l'. If there is an 'l' at the beginning of the word, he will pronounce it as an 'r'. This has to do with the way the Korean alphabet and its corresponding pronunciation rules are set up. The Korean alphabet possesses a character that is a combination r/l sound depending on where it is placed in a Korean word. For example, for Koreans speaking English, 'Rice' becomes 'Lice', and 'Clock' becomes 'Crock'. Of course, this contributes to the everlasting confusion of the Western English teacher, who will spend months with the Korean student trying to repair his pronunciation. I'll spare going through my dozen or so stories involving humorous mispronunciations, however, there are a few worth mentioning.

A friend and co-worker of mine, Jane, and another friend of ours, Jack, ran into a variety of comical communication episodes during their time living and working in Korea. Once, a Korean woman whose English was difficult to understand said to Jack, "Jane is a tough girl! She loves crime!" Of course, it took Jack time to process this comment before asking the woman, "What do you mean she loves crime? Is she a criminal? A gangster?" Well, it took a good five minutes or so for Jack to realize that the woman was trying to say that Jane is a tough girl because she likes to *climb*. Jane was a mountain climber. It all made sense to him after some quick clarification. Sometime after, another woman who was a friend of Jack's said to him, "Jack, when you first come to Korea, you didn't smell, but now you smell all the time." Of course, Jack didn't know how to take this comment. He thought about it for a few moments before responding with, "Thanks, I guess." When he pressed for her to explain, she stated that in the beginning, Jack "frowned all the time," but now, he "smells." With Jack's patience and savvy understanding, acquired by a whole year living and communicating with Korean people, he realized that the woman was trying to say, "*smiles*" not "smells." Supposedly, when Jack first came to Korea, he never smiled, but now, he smiled all the time.

Communication, overall, is an absolute challenge in Korea, especially upon first arrival. However, not being able to communicate at first brings out a certain 'power' in a person. You start out by having to work very hard to communicate the simplest things, using a lot of nonverbal communication and hand gestures, and learning how to resolve miscommunications the best way you possibly can. But it can make you stronger in a way that increases your communication capabilities and heightens your senses. You even begin predicting communication problems and solving them before the communication even takes place. I slightly understood what people were asking of me and what they wanted of me, just by paying attention to the look on their face or listening to the inflection of their voice—even though I didn't understand the language. Early on in my contract before I understood any Korean, a man on the bus turned around and began speaking to me. I didn't understand ninety percent of what he was saying, but I found myself naturally answering him as if I did understand him. I simply listened to the words I *did* understand, and responded according to what I thought he was asking. I don't think I realized I was doing this, and he seemed satisfied with my short answers. I have reason to believe he asked where I was going, because in the middle of his long sentence I heard the Korean word for "where." I replied

"Vivien," which is the name of the bus stop near my apartment. He nodded, then pointed in the direction of the university across the field and rattled off another question, which again, I only understood about ten percent of. I figured he was asking me if I was a student at the university, because that is what people often ask me when I tell them that I live near it. I answered no. Again, he was satisfied with my answer. I had no idea if what I think he said was correct, but I heard key words and read body language that suggested he was asking me where I lived and if I was a student. Overall, I strongly believe that one's communication capabilities are greatly enhanced after being placed in a situation which requires working hard to communicate and finding any way to get the message across.

Korean vs. Western Values in the Classroom

Sometimes cultural differences can be frustrating, especially in a professional environment. Even for someone like me, who has spent my graduate school years psychologically preparing myself for my days of travel and coping with foreign environments and cultural differences. I know that the children I taught were exactly that—just children. They didn't understand that I was trying to teach them something. They had energetic minds that wanted to play all day, and if they were bored they were not afraid to show it by misbehaving. It was so frustrating for me to teach children because my patience was often nonexistent, and I was always afraid of losing control.

When I worked at the kindergarten I often wondered what these children's parents' expectations were when they sent their kids off to a foreign language school. It is true that the kindergarten years are some of the most influential academic years of a child's life. What needs to be remembered by Western English teachers teaching children in Korea is that they are teaching in an English language school (or an English language department) with a staff that consciously and unconsciously teaches Western values for six to seven hours a day. It's not only about the English. I often wondered if parents realize this when they drop their children off at school every day. Do they realize that their children will be learning about individuality, which is a Western characteristic, and Halloween, which has never been celebrated in Korea before? The answer is yes and no. Sending one's children to a private English language academy in Korea is sometimes a sign of status and prestige. The tuition is usually not cheap and the value of learning English is clearly understood by Korean parents who obsess over their children's education. Some parents realize that their children will learn many of the Western values that the Western English teacher brings into the classroom, and they are fine with that. They must be if they want their children to learn from a native English speaker, and having Western values slipped into a daily lesson is virtually unavoidable. I must say, however, that a lot of what the children learn at home does tend to stick with them while they're at school. For example, during my contract at the kindergarten, a child in the school hit a slightly older child in the face. At the time, I didn't know why. It was sometimes a mystery when a child became angry or began to cry because they could not explain what happened due to the language barrier. Anyhow, the older child never hit the younger child back, and did not even, in the least bit, stick up for himself. The child later confessed to a teacher that the reason he did not hit the younger child back was because he was exactly that— younger. Korean children are taught in the home to respect anyone who is older than they are, but they are especially taught to be patient with anyone who is younger than them. Respect them, and if they do you harm, do not harm them in return. I saw this 'age respect' mentality among most of the children in our school. In Western culture, many Westerners have an 'eye for an eye' mentality in which age is not an issue when there is a dispute. Since Korean children in English-speaking schools are exposed to Westerners and Western values, you would think that the 'age respect' mentality would begin to peter out. In my country, children don't stop to think whether or not the child that just hit them is older or younger. They just swing back. Of course, I cannot generalize and say that this is true in all cases involving children in my country, just like I cannot say that all Korean children stop to think about the age of the other child before they decide to defend themselves. There are some exceptions. In my experience teaching hundreds of children in Korean classrooms, I saw that this 'age respect' attitude was often demonstrated by very young Korean children. I saw Western teachers encourage their children to fight back no matter what the circumstances were (or what the ages were) of the children who physically offended them. It didn't have to be fighting back *physically* either. A verbal comeback would have sufficed. I even saw a Western teacher bite a child on the hand because that child had bitten other children on the hand. The teacher wanted him to know how painful it felt. It was clear that Western teachers needed to learn how to recognize and understand Korean values learned in the home and the values that parents wished to preserve in their children, so that they could better preserve those values in their own classrooms. There is a way to incorporate both Korean and Western values in daily activities and classroom management without the two conflicting. It is certainly possible to have a happy medium. I also noticed that some Western teachers continued teaching as if they were in a Western classroom (which does not work well), and parents did take notice to this. But just as expected, and in typical Korean fashion, Korean parents will always assume that the teacher knows best, and they will (almost) never question what their children learn (or how they learn) in the classroom.

Western English teachers and Korean staff sometimes have conflicting ideas regarding how the classroom and school is being run, what values are being taught, and what the overall priorities are. This creates conflict and leaves the Korean boss insisting it should be his way and the English teacher insisting it should be *his* way. It is very challenging to resolve these kinds of conflicts which often do not get resolved at all. The following excerpts are anonymous blurbs I found on the Internet. They seem to have been written for both Westerners and Korean bosses, and offer a glimpse into what the Westerner perceives are differences between Korean and Western values. The first comment by Roy addresses miscommunication issues between foreign teachers and Korean managers in hagwons. It's good advice for both the Western teacher and the director. The second comment by FixerH is a warning about the school (Language Institute) that he worked for. It addresses the horrors he encountered while teaching there. It is only one of many realities that Western teachers sometimes face when working in Korea, however, I advise not to let FixerH's comments scare you. Individuals who are thinking about pursuing a teaching career in Korea should always do extensive research on the schools they plan to apply for and exercise caution when needed.

Here is Roy's comment:

> *'After reading some comments by both hagwon managers and teachers and having observed what has happened in my own experience, I thought I might add a few comments. Western teachers, especially American teachers, want a sense of professionalism. A common complaint is lack of organization. This is a big problem for teachers who don't have English language teaching experience. To go somewhere where you don't have books, the course structure changes all the time and students are mixed at many levels, can be difficult. For an inexperienced teacher this can present problems. Imagine this for a recent college graduate with no work experience in a foreign country. Koreans (from observation) value interpersonal relationships. These are the gifts and other things that bosses do for the teachers. This is where when a teacher is unhappy, the boss buys them dinner rather than fix the problem at work. From observation, this annoys the Korean teachers as much as the Western teachers. But what we are seeing is a culturally specific response to an organizational problem. The problem is that what the Western teacher expects and what the hagwon expects are different. For hagwons, remember, you have to manage your teachers. That means you have to manage young teachers with no experience. Management is not about telling people what to do, but making sure they have the resources to their job. Without those resources, they will not care about the teaching. They will go out and get drunk, come to class late and*

so on. If they get fired, they don't care. You also have to remember that Koreans, due to their neo-confucianist past, have an attitude to rules and contracts that is fairly flexible. It is not quite the same as the Chinese. The worst insult to a Chinese person is to insist on following the rules. Koreans are similar but not quite the same. Western people don't understand this. A great insult to a Western person is to not follow the rules or terms of a contract. This appears to be one of the major areas of contention.....people fighting over contracts and hagwons seeing the rules as flexible. The solution is simple. Most people will work hard if you reward them for working hard. That reward does not need to be money, but should follow the terms of the contract. Bad bosses always give the hardest workers the most work.....punishing those who work hard. Rather, a good boss is there to support their hard workers. Give them the resources that they need. Don't treat them like a star...it will just go their heads.....but make sure they don't need anything when it comes to doing their job. Remember communication is the key to your business. Leave it chance and the teachers won't know what the hagwon wants and the hagwon won't know what the teachers want or need. So, the whole relationship breaks down. In frustration, teachers do the midnight run and managers go mad, yelling, screaming, and ripping the teachers off. Anyway that is my view on this matter.....there are simple solutions in the workplace so everyone can be happy.' - "Roy"

In my experience working in several hagwons, Roy's perceptions are accurate. Many hagwon owners (and Korean staff) do not know how to make their Western teachers happy, and mistakenly assume that the Westerners will hold the same values as Koreans. What seems obvious to the Western teacher, such as the boss making sure the teacher has necessary materials to do his job, may not be so obvious (or important) to the boss. Of course, the contract being seen as flexible is too often a problem for foreign English teachers who expect that the terms of their employment be honored and respected. This is a value interpretation problem *and* a communication problem. When the boss tinkers with the terms of the contract, it's not always to take advantage of the teacher. He may be doing something that he thinks may benefit or please the teacher. Of course, this is incomprehensible to the teacher who accuses the boss of changing terms (sometimes verbally) without notice to benefit himself or his business. The best way to get around this problem is to make it clear when accepting a teaching job that you expect the terms of the contract to be honored and unchanged. It's always best to read your contract inside and out and make sure that both parties understand it. Sometimes a hagwon or school director (or recruiter) will print out a standardized teaching contract found on the internet and give it to the English teacher without fully reading it himself. In this case, the contract is a mere 'technicality' that needs to be gotten out of the way. But of course, unbeknownst to the school director, the English teacher places a great deal of meaning and weight on the contract. So, it is important to make sure the school director knows exactly how valuable the contract is to you. This may make him actually read every word printed on it. This certainly would prevent problems in the future. A lot has changed since 2003 and 2004, and the Korean government (and immigration) now has divisions with English speakers to help with contract problems and miscommunications between foreign workers and Korean companies. This includes problems between English teachers and Korean bosses.

The following is FixerH's comment that serves as more of a complaint. In my opinion, it is the far extreme of what normally happens when taking on teaching jobs in Korea.

> 'I quit Language Institute because of the lack of fairness and business sense at Language Institute resulting from the fact that the owner and his little brother are incompetent, and they don't treat their teachers like human beings. They treat their teachers like game pieces that they use to make money, and that's it. I left mainly for the following reasons:
> 1. My boss didn't pay into the National Medical Coverage Plan for me, and when I asked him where my National Medical Coverage Card (Bohum Card) was, he lied to me and told me there is no such thing in Korea. Furthermore, when I asked him why he lied to me a few months after the fact, he lied to me again by saying that he didn't lie to me in the first place. He did this more than once. 2. He was charging me rent, which is not standard for hagwons to do—and moreover, for an insect-infested apartment with no air conditioning and poor insulation that's located a half an hour away from the school. 3. The teachers' salary (1.8 million Won per month) is lower than that of any of the other foreign teachers that I met in Busan. That's not OK, especially since my boss didn't provide me with free housing. Also, he charged me a housing deposit, and I had to commute 2 hours a day on crowded buses because my apartment was so far away (and I was working a split shift). 4. My boss tried to stick me with a roommate at least three times even though I made it clear from the start that I didn't want a roommate, and my apartment was too small for two people. 5. I was lied to before I came to Korea about what I would be making for interviews, and when I

informed my boss of this once I got to Korea, he chose to ignore me. 6. I strongly suspect that my boss pocketed my taxes that he took from my paycheck. He never gave me any paperwork to suggest otherwise, and I shouldn't have had to ask to see any either. 7. My boss repeatedly refused to be reasonable and decent when teachers were negotiating their contracts. On occasion, he even rejected every condition that a teacher asked for. 8. He withheld the following money from me, which he would not pay me unless I finished my contract: the pension money that he deducted from my paycheck, my severance pay, the housing deposit, my vacation pay, and the cost of my flight home. This was one of his ways of forcing me to stay at Language Institute and trying to force me to put up with his abuse. (Severance pay is equal to one month's salary, and it is the law that an employer must pay it to his/her employee once he/she has completed twelve months of work.) 9. There was a total lack of organization in his managing. It seems that as soon as a new teacher was hired at Language Institute, another one quit or was fired. Having teachers come and go all the time creates an unstable and unorganized working environment. 10. My boss has repeatedly waited to the last minute to make decisions, which has always cost the school more money and caused everyone at the school to experience unnecessary stress. My boss changed the vacation days for August with hardly any advanced notice time. That made it difficult for the teachers to plan vacations. He cancelled the seminar day the day before it was to have taken place. If I had known that I would have that day off, then I could have planned a three-day trip to Seoul or some other place. 11. He continuously makes bad decisions in how he chooses to put money into the school. For the example, why do the students need new lockers and a big screen TV in the lobby when one of the computers in the teachers' room often gets a floppy disk stuck in it? You would think that my boss would realize that only having one copy machine that works for a whole office full of teachers causes a lot of unnecessary stress for his teachers. I could go on. 12. My boss has showed horrible judgment in whom he has chosen to give power over his teachers on numerous occasions. 13. My boss repeatedly showed bad judgment in his hiring practices by hiring people, who don't have the adequate qualifications and experience to be exceptional teachers. This means that he has been lying to the students by making them think that they are getting an excellent education, when in fact they are not. 14. My boss was charging teenage kids 40,000 Won per hour for private lessons and he was only paying the teachers 16,500 Won per hour to teach these

> *kids. 15. My boss did not pay me for overtime work, which included 15 extra hours of work during the month of August helping him with human resources. He even had me come in to work on Sunday and didn't pay me for it. 16. My boss tried not to pay one of his former teachers his severance pay.' -"FixerH"*

Obviously, FixerH's boss held no values whatsoever, and was behaving in a very shady and un-Korean manner. It is important to remember that not all teachers experience what FixerH has experienced, and there are teachers that love their jobs (and Korea) so much that they have been living and working in Korea for many years. Not all bosses are crooked as well. FixerH could have easily hired an English-speaking attorney and would have probably won if a lawsuit was pursued. There are so many factors that come into play when a venture succeeds or fails, and of course, nothing is ever set in stone. This is especially true when accepting a teaching job in Korea. If you feel that the job is not working out, or there are things that dissatisfy you and that you feel are irreparable, there is no reason why you shouldn't be able to give sufficient notice and be on your way back home. You may have to reimburse your employer for airfare, but you may resign at any time. In no way should you be obligated to pay extra fees or allow the boss to confiscate your passport or anything else for that matter. Don't ever let a Korean boss 'muscle' you. As a foreign English teacher in Korea, you have rights. There are plenty of organizations and law firms in Korea to ensure that everything is within its legal boundaries regarding your employment.

In my opinion, if you have a chance to come to Korea as a tourist first before accepting a teaching job, then do it. Foreigners are normally allowed a thirty day stay in Korea as a tourist and this is plenty of time to travel around the country, explore different cities and neighborhoods, and scope out possible schools of interest that are hiring Western English teachers. If thirty days is not enough, then you can obtain a three month tourist visa (six months for Canadians). Three months is sufficient time to get a feel for the culture, figure out what communication hurdles you will face, and decide which schools have good and bad reputations. Overall, discovering if living and working in Korea is right for you is best done by experiencing it first instead of signing a contract for a school you know nothing about.

My first question for FixerH would have been, "What did your contract say?" Were the terms of his pay, his overtime pay, his rental charge, etc., in the terms of the contract? If they weren't, why did he sign it? If they were, and the boss verbally changed the terms after the contract was signed, why didn't FixerH obtain help? As previously stated, fairness and labor laws are issues for foreign workers in Korea, and there are divisions within the government and immigration (as well as attorneys) who can help with these issues. They can clarify laws and act to resolve conflicts between the foreign worker and Korean manager. Again, as long as the terms in the contract are specific, problems like FixerH's can be avoided. Also, if you can't visit the school immediately, I always recommend talking to other Western teachers who are or have been employed by the school you are interested in working at. It is a good idea to get a 'feel' for how foreign staff is treated and if the environment is fair, happy, and satisfactory. Some important questions to ask Western staff are if the terms of everyone's contract are honored, if they perceive the atmosphere as being organized, and if there is open communication between foreign staff and Korean management. If the school director won't disclose contact details for current or past staff, then there is probably something wrong. Check the school's reputation. There are blacklists available online that list schools with damaged reputations due to mismanagement or mistreatment of staff. If there is a repeated problem with a particular chain of schools, the rumor tends to get around Korea quickly. Pay attention to rumors and investigate them. You can't afford to ignore certain things. There are plenty of Westerners in Korea that will be happy to answer your questions and give you advice about living and working in Korea, and what you should and shouldn't expect. Dave's ESL café website (www.davesesl cafe.com) has a chat/posting board for foreign teachers in Korea as well as many other countries. Take advantage of these boards and ask as many questions as you can.

Coping With Your Job

If you work with children, trying to discipline and teach three, four, and five-year-olds can get the best of any teacher, whether or not a language barrier exists. There was a point at the English kindergarten where I lost all of my patience, understanding, and motivation. I was beyond frustration. I was at my brink. My students were not listening to me and they were grossly misbehaving. Worst of all, they were disrespecting all of the teachers. It was absolute devastation, especially for me being a beginning teacher. I lost all control. I just didn't seem to click with the children I was teaching. My boss and fellow co-workers began to sense there was something wrong. After a few weeks of going off the deep end, my support system became concerned about me and decided to lend me a helping hand. Luckily, there was a solution, and I had my co-workers to thank for coming up with it. Since Jane's students were a bit older and better behaved than mine, we decided to switch classes so that I could teach her students and she could teach mine. After all, Jane was much better with singing and playing kids' games than I was. I strongly believed she was a better match for the younger students. Jane was also much better with disciplining children. I, on the other hand, worked much better with older children who were more likely to respond to my organized English lessons. After my co-workers and I addressed the idea of the switch to the Korean boss, the boss obliged. He realized that he would be risking student-teacher harmony and possibly my resignation if he didn't agree with the switch. The pressure was on him, and luckily, he responded to us. This is an excellent example of how one's support system can make an impact on the way someone copes with a situation. My co-workers were concerned about my emotional ability to handle my students and they were determined to find a solution to my problem. They didn't want to see me resign. That touched me a great deal. After that, I was much better able to cope with my working environment.

Coping with unmotivated and misbehaved students can be an enormous morale breaker, and in an elementary English school classroom (or hagwon) the foreign teacher can expect plenty of unmotivated students who lack the drive or the energy to even keep their heads off their desks. An unmotivated class causes an unmotivated teacher, and the attitudes of the two definitely affect each other. Of course, I had unmotivated students in both of my kindergarten and elementary classes, especially during my first contract, but the lack of motivation among some of my elementary students was truly unbelievable. Some of my eight to eleven-year-olds often whined and threw fits whenever I would begin a new lesson. I spent a lot of time and effort creating a quality lesson plan that was organized and so full of relevant information, and all the students wanted to do was play. How could I be motivated enough to teach my lessons if my class wasn't motivated enough to learn them? This was a major problem. I didn't know how to cope. What was even worse was when I tried to take my boss' advice when he said, "Just ignore the unmotivated ones!" It was then that I realized that doing this would completely take the point out of teaching. Sometimes, I felt that what I was doing was worthless.

After a few months of sheer frustration, I was exhausted. However, I started to understand why the students were always so tired, whiny and unmotivated. Like I mentioned before, students are in school all day, sometimes eleven hours or more. This can be quite a load for a young child that wants to play all day. After a full day of studying, these children were, no doubt, too exhausted to study by the time they came to my classroom. In my classroom, they desired a release from the day's work. That explained why they had no desire to learn English.

The strategy I developed to cope with this cycle of pushing overloaded children to learn more involved a lot of creativity. I had to be innovative with my lesson planning, incorporating a lot of English games and activities that taught what needed to be taught, but at the same time, served as a release for overworked children. I also had to make sure I kept lecture to a minimum.

Being more creative and designing relevant games for the students kept everyone happy. It kept the children behaved and motivated and it kept me confident and alive in the classroom. It also kept the boss from fearing that parents would withdraw their children from the school because English "wasn't fun." After I started doing this, it wasn't long before I saw a change in the atmosphere and a positive change in the energy of the students.

Situations at work aren't the only things that affect how a foreign teacher copes with his job. Everyday living situations play a huge role in learning how to cope. A teacher comes a long way from the familiarities of his home when he comes to Korea to teach. He must encompass a new environment with all new stresses. Not only does the foreigner have to cope with a new country and the people in it, but he must also cope with a new job. If teaching is not quite his profession, than he must cope with a job he has no experience doing. A few months into my first contract there was a fire that viciously swept through the apartment building where the other teachers and I had been living. The fire was a severe interruption in my daily life as well as in my adjustment process. It affected all of the teachers in my school. Immediately after the fire, my morale sunk. It was the lowest it had ever been during my first six months teaching in Korea. After the fire, I came home everyday to an apartment that was dark, smoky, and covered with ash and soot. For two weeks I suffered from headaches from the fumes, and I felt that my Korean boss did very little to sooth the physical and emotional devastation of what had happened. Of course, for him, business had to be carried on as usual. I also felt like trying to do my job was impossible. Just trying to focus on the children during the day, knowing I had to come home to an apartment full of burned belongings, was devastating. How did I cope? Understanding that there was not much I could do about the situation other than wait for the landlord to get the building back in order, once again, I relied on my support system of co-workers. Since most of my fellow Western teachers lived in the same building, we all experienced the same crisis, therefore, we understood how to console each other. Of course, the odds of this situation happening are extremely rare, so my intention is not to scare potential teachers in any way. I do, however, want to emphasize once again that the best way to cope with anything negative that may happen to you in terms of your job, serious or not, is to consult and develop a tight relationship with your fellow co-workers. The value of this to your emotional well-being cannot be stressed enough.

Chapter 7:
Business as Usual

The Business Side of the Korean English School

In the beginning of my first contract, the school had a massive thanksgiving party at a *TGIF* restaurant nearby. The party was for the staff, children, and the children's parents, and was more massive than I ever thought it would be. All of the school's kindergarten students and their mothers (many times mothers are housewives, therefore, unlike working fathers, they have time to attend their children's school affairs) came to eat American food—spaghetti, chicken, baked potatoes, and French fries. I was actually looking forward to this day up until I started to realize (early that morning) how chaotic it was going to be. Of course, all of the Western teachers were told at the last minute by the director that we would have to do the speaking, entertaining, and meeting and greeting with the parents. This was a lot more complicated than it sounds, especially when we had no time to mentally prepare. Some of the Western teaching staff at the school strongly disliked meeting with the parents, only because of the communication and cultural barriers they would have to encounter. Having to explain to a parent who doesn't speak English how her son or daughter is doing in school is absolutely painstaking!. Why did the Western teachers have to do this and not the Korean teaching staff? That is a great question. After all, the Korean teachers could communicate better with the parents. Evidently, the boss had intended to coordinate this Thanksgiving event, not as a nice day out, but as an advertising opportunity to market his teachers and his school. Unbeknownst to the entire Western teaching staff, he was using us as marketing tools. After all, he was a businessman not an educator, and his past actions have dictated that. I have come to understand that, in Korea, if you are an employee of a company you are a representative of that company, and you can be used in any way to market the company and its products usually without your consent. Of course, not all of that is legal, but it is a silent expectation of the employees by management. I realized that this is especially true for English academies and hagwons. However, if a director has a good understanding of the Western mind and what his foreign employees will accept and not accept, he will most likely not subject his staff to being the main attraction at such a circus of an event. At the time of the event, the Western staff was thinking, *"what a nice boss, he's taking us all out for TGIF dinner—just to be nice!"* In fact, his intentions weren't so, even though he wanted us to think it. Of course, the Western staff ended up running around the restaurant all day, performing last minute dramas on etiquette and the history of thanksgiving, getting the kids to sing songs, and (worst of all) meeting with the parents to explain what was going on with their children's classes. You can argue that the reason why the boss didn't properly inform the Western staff in advance about their duties at this function was because he was stressed or just caught up in last minute organizing. It could have been because he didn't want to alarm us about what was about to happen. It could have also been because he felt that he did not need to inform us at all about the details of the event.

    As was mentioned before, the contents of an employment contract (or any other contract for that matter) is often flexible in Korea. It can also be altered by the employer and employee at any time with the consent of both parties. Of course, many English school employers understand that Westerners expect a solid contract in which terms are honored, therefore, they (the employers) do their best to keep it that way. Sometimes, English school contracts are deliberately written in vague terms just so they can be manipulated later. I advise to stay away from a vague contract, or request that it be revised. There will occasionally be duties you are expected to perform that have not been detailed in your contract. They are considered standard duties of a Western teacher and will usually involve participating in off-campus school events and having conferences with parents. I agree, it is difficult to specify every nook and cranny of what a teacher is required to do. Of course, the contract I signed at my first school didn't say anything about having to entertain parents at functions. It was implied though, that employees were required to participate in any school activities. The *TGIF* affair was a 'school activity'. This is where the flexibility kicks in. The contract also didn't state that Western employees can automatically be used as marketing tools for the company at any time. I have reason to believe that this rule is an 'unwritten Korean business rule', as are many rules in Korea.

I heard of a Western English teacher who took a trip to his local city of Busan for a weekend and shockingly saw his face on the side of a bus advertising the school that he worked for. He never gave consent for this, but even though he was embarrassed, he took it with stride. I'm not sure if this story is true, but it sounds likely. I do know that many English teachers have seen their faces on flyers and in catalogues, and have never consented to any of it! One new English teacher arrived for his first day at a rival school of mine only to find a grossly huge banner pinned up on the front of the school's building with his face on it. It read, "Welcome Randy!" For foreign teachers who have been working in Korea for a long time, this 'violation' of personal property seems like a fact of life, and seeing their faces on billboards and in magazines is not surprising to them anymore.

The English school in Korea can be a cut-throat business, full of negotiation, hierarchy, unwritten rules, and sometimes, a lot of disorganization. The English hagwon can be an enormous money-maker, and there is definitely never a shortage of English schools and hagwons (as there is never a shortage of English teaching jobs for Westerners). If an individual is accustomed to the Western style of business practice, the Korean-style business can be quite a challenge to get accustomed to. Verbal miscommunication, flexibility in time, inefficiency and lack of materials can discourage a Western teacher. It's often forgotten by the Korean employer that it is the Western teacher that makes his business successful, and sometimes Western teachers are rarely given appropriate credit for the success a business achieves. Of course, there are other factors that play into the success of a (school) business, including location, size, and curriculum. But for the English school in Korea, Western English teachers play an enormous part in terms of success. Korean parents often will only send their children to an English school that employs a native English speaker, as opposed to an English school with Korean English teachers who speak excellent English. Rival English hagwons can be competitive with each other in terms of hiring Western staff. Sometimes, hagwon directors will favor and give preference to light skinned, blue-eyed teachers, feeling confident that the physically stereo-typical Westerner will attract better business. Physical appearance, weight, and age disappointingly seem to be high priority for many English schools during the hiring process. This is why they always ask for a recent photo to be submitted along with the resume. Unfortunately, many small town schools are still not open to hiring people of color. Of course, this is not always the case, so don't let this discourage you if you don't fit the stereo-type. There are plenty of teaching jobs for all types of Westerners, regardless of appearance, weight, age, and race.

The following is an excellent example of a cut-throat move on the part of a Korean business. It is the story of my Korean friend and what he thought would finally be a suitable job for him. Kwan-Hyub had a job that just wasn't working out for him. He didn't make the salary he thought he deserved; therefore, he quit and found another job as a salesman for a well known company. Before he was hired, he and his future boss participated in a salary negotiation that guaranteed him a minimum salary, however, it would not be decided what that minimum was until later—perhaps a month later—after he would get hired. Seeing that he didn't have many job options at the time, Kwan-Hyub took the job and agreed to meet with his boss some time later to discuss what his salary would be. A month or so later, Kwan-Hyub met again with his boss who stated that the salary hadn't been determined yet, and informed Kwan-Hyub that he would not get paid until it has been determined. So, Kwan-Hyub worked a second month without a salary. After the second month, he met with his boss once again. Unfortunately, the boss had *still* not decided on what his salary would be. Of course, Kwan-Hyub voiced his dissatisfaction with this the best that he could. Suspicious of this boss' motives and angry that he had already put in so much time and effort to the company, Kwan-Hyub quit the job in his third month and moved on to a new job search. It was never clear if he ever received any pay whatsoever. Most likely, he didn't. Of course, Kwan-Hyub could have consulted with a labor attorney regarding the issue and perhaps even pressed charges. However, he should have done that immediately after the first month, and more importantly, he should have never signed the contract without understanding what his minimum salary would be. Lesson noted: do not ever accept a position without your salary set and written in your contract. In addition, never permit a change in salary terms *after* the contract has been signed (unless it has been a year and you're up for renegotiation). School directors are running a business and business operators can be sneaky!

Corruption

Just like in Western countries, corruption in business is rampant in Korea, especially in the English school business. The second company I worked for required that I visit people's homes and give them private English lessons. This, in fact, is illegal in Korea. Under no circumstances are foreigners allowed to travel to people's homes and give individual lessons in English. As stated before, all English teachers working in Korea must also have at least a Bachelor's degree in any subject in order to teach English (and in order to receive the E2 visa). These laws are crystal clear. However, the company I worked for during my second contract continuously employed teachers illegally without a college or university degree, and included private English lessons on the teachers' schedules. How did the company get away with this? According to the company's own manager, the company consistently paid off immigration to keep quiet and look the other way, and to disregard who the company was employing. So, why would Westerners apply for this company if it is a well-known fact that what they would be doing is illegal? Because foreign English teachers without a degree can have a chance to gain valuable teaching experience abroad and make good money. As far as I know, very few jobs are available in Korea to Westerners who only have a high school education except illegal ones. Also, it seemed like Westerners who worked for this kind of English school/company were guaranteed by their bosses a certain amount of protection from immigration. At least, that is what the Korean bosses made their Western staff believe. Of course, some (not many) Korean people understand that foreigners teaching English privately is illegal, but they contribute to these illegal businesses by hiring the teachers anyway due to the high demand for learning English! So, in the end Everyone is happy; the boss, the parent, the illegal English teacher—at least until the teacher doesn't get paid by the boss. When this happens, there is nowhere to run. The teacher cannot complain to immigration, because he would then have to admit he is working illegally! At this point, the teacher's only options would be to grin and bear it or quit.

In an online article by Kim Myoung-Soo entitled *'Causes of Corruption and Irregularities'*, the source of corruption in Korea is detailed. She states that corruption is synonymous to disease, and corruption, as well as disease, plagues every society in one way or another.

> *'In Korea, corruption is so deep-rooted and pervasive that literally no segment of society is free from its dark shadow. The country's political circles have long lost the people's trust due to their frequent incidences of corruption, and hardly any public office is free from irregularities of some kind, though the extent may vary. Government offices especially vulnerable to corruption include police and tax offices, as well as those involved with the issuance of licenses, formulation of policy guidelines and regulations, and procurement. As seen in the case involving collusion between several sitting judges and lawyers, even the nation's judiciary is susceptible to corruption. Meanwhile, Koreans were once again dismayed by reports of widespread irregularities in the government's handling of military conscription and arms procurement programs. Even education is not immune from corrupt practices, as revealed in the bribery incident related to the appointment of a professor at prestigious Seoul National University.'* -*'Kim Myoung-Soo'*

Kim Myoung-Soo details where she believes corruption lies and the reasons for corruption. She is careful to mention that some of the following causes are more involved than others. Among the causes she states are: 1. lack of effective anti-corruption measures, 2. lack of independence of anti-corruption agencies, 3. lack of consistency and fairness, 4. career politicians and costly political structure, 5. the presence of authoritarian regimes, 6. lack of sufficient punishment, 7. excessive government regulation, 8. meager salaries, 9. presence of an ambiguous definition of corruption, 10. confused sense of values, 11. competitive consumption, and 12. slack attitude toward corruption. Kim concludes that overall, it is "a variety of political, administrative, economic, social, psychological, and cultural circumstances," that affects corruption[8]. I believe that it is exactly some of these factors that are responsible for corruption in some Korean English schools. In the case of the illegally operating English schools and the illegal practices of Korean employers, it is understood that they can, most likely, get away with it due to lack of regulation and consequences. It is also possible that the directors and owners simply may not think they are doing anything illegal whatsoever (ambiguous definition of corruption). Also, Korean businesses can take advantage of the foreigner who does not understand the legal system and what actions are legal and illegal. This reverts back to the idea of if the foreign employee does not understand what he is entitled to, especially concerning pay and benefits, the employer is more likely to take advantage of him. If the foreign employee doesn't understand that his employer is taking part in corrupt practices, the business will most likely get away with it because there is no one to 'let the cat out of the bag'. It can also be said that the English business can most likely get away with illegal practices due to the extremely high demand of English education. This is the 'competitive consumption' factor of the business. However, this can also be the exact reason why English businesses *cannot* get away with illegal practices. If the English business is so competitive and in high demand, it may just as well be tightly regulated and closely watched by immigration and the government. Lesson noted: know your rights and what you are entitled to, keep your eyes open, and never feel obligated to 'play along' with a corrupt school or boss.

English Teaching Contracts: What You Need to Know

The vagueness I talked about earlier in regards to Korean English school teaching contracts, in reality, can occasionally work to the Westerner's advantage. Sometimes it does and sometimes it doesn't. My first contract was miswritten in a way where it stated that after I complete my twelve month contract I will receive a "severance pay equal to the last three months' total salary." This sounded to me like I would receive a total of three months' salary after I complete my year working. However, later I learned that the Korean individual who wrote the contract meant that the amount of my severance pay would be calculated by taking the *average of each month's salary* I received (during the last three months). The missing word in the original contract's clause was *average*. Of course, I came to Korea thinking that I would receive a huge payout after I finished my contract. This was a mistake that could have possibly worked to my advantage in my own country if I were to legally pursue it. However, everyone in Korea knows that severance is always equal to one month's pay. There is no arguing about it. I wanted to reason that I was entitled to a six million won (I made two million per month) severance pay and hope that my director would honor it since it was clearly stated in the contract. Of course, that's a fat chance!

It is important to understand that all schools in Korea are required by law to pay the foreign English teacher a severance of at least one month's salary as long as the contract is fulfilled. Some employers try to get around this and offer a free trip anywhere in Asia at the completion of a contract in Lieu of the severance. I advise not to take this offer only because purchasing a travel package anywhere in Asia is much cheaper for the employer than paying out a severance. If you want to go on a trip anywhere in Asia, it's best to accept the severance and pay for the trip yourself. You may have plenty of severance money left over.

Most English teaching contracts (as well as many other employment contracts) in Korea are to be considered a 'rough working copy'. As I said before, it is sometimes regarded as flexible (more often by the employer), and can often be mutually verbally negotiated and changed by the director or the teacher. Of course, I recommend against any verbal changes. In my experience, hagwon directors will just send you a standard contract downloaded from the internet, and many times, they don't even know what's really in it. They just fill in the important matters such as hours, pay, contract period, benefits, housing, and taxes and overtime. The rest is standard contract fare. That doesn't mean, however, that you shouldn't take the contract seriously and go through it with a fine-tooth comb. In my experience, it has been extremely helpful in the long run to request that the contract be very specific. This has saved me from many misunderstandings with my director. Don't be afraid, upon review of your contract, to change something in the contract or rewrite something that needs to be more specific. Just notify your recruiter and/or director and tell them of the changes before both parties sign. However, the changes should be requested verbally before you begin rewriting sections of the contract. For example, my recruiter didn't notice that my housing was listed as a single room studio in my contract, even though I had already discussed the housing needs due to my dogs and cat moving in with me. I went ahead and changed it to what we had discussed, which was a minimum two bedroom apartment or home. Other things such as pay, hours, or overtime can be easily confused as well if it is not detailed in the contract.

On the Dave's ESL Cafe website (www.daveseslcafe.com), there is helpful information for English teachers and prospective English teachers. On the site there is a typical employment contract. The contents of this contract are what can generally be expected when applying for English teaching jobs. I believe that one can distinguish a really good teaching job from an average one (or bad one) by the contents and the professionalism of the contract. As I said before, a simple and vague contract can determine if the terms can be easily manipulated by the employer.

The main components that should be in an English teaching contract are as follows: salary, housing, hours, class size, travel reimbursement, taxes, insurance, and severance pay. Of course most of these can be negotiated (except for taxes).

The contracts posted below are normally used as a general template for English teachers seeking jobs at children's schools and hagwons. Again, it is a rough working copy and can be specifically changed and suited to the position applied for. It is not what every teaching contract will look like. I have included my own comments in between the contract clauses of the first contract. These comments are in italics so that you can distinguish them from the contents of the contract. The second contract is a simpler contract and was actually used for my third place of employment. You will see that it is not as detailed and thorough as the first contract. Also, if you decide to use these contract templates, any blanks must be filled in according to the agreements between the potential English teacher (you) and the school director.

Example of the First Teaching Contract:

EMPLOYMENT AGREEMENT

THIS EMPLOYMENT AGREEMENT is made between Mr./Mrs...................... the owner of .... School hereafter referred to as 'employer', and English Instructor Mr./Ms. ....hereafter referred to as 'employee'.

This EMPLOYMENT AGREEMENT has been made firm, this ...... day of ..../..........
The points of this contract cannot be renegotiated during its term.
Conditions of this Contract:

1. TREATMENT & RESPONSIBILITIES
We, the employer and the employee are individuals of equal human value and will treat each other as such. We sign this contract so to harmoniously and respectfully exchange our services as agreed upon here.

The service of the employee is to offer work in the way that is agreed upon here. The employer will return the employee's work, with providing a peaceful and respectful work environment, and also with material and service supports such as housing, salary, medical insurance, etc, as agreed upon in this contract.

> *Shady: If the contract reads "the employee will follow the instructions of the management in ..._____", and then an empty space follows, it can be a recipe for disaster. The contract does not specify what the management will ask you to do if the blank is left empty.*

2- GUARANTEED WORKLOAD, HOURS, DAYS

The Guaranteed workload is maximum of ___ clock hours per week, or ___ clock hours (also equal to ___ classes of ___ minutes each), per 4 weeks or 1 month 'Pay Period'. The 'guaranteed hours' means that the employee's minimum salary remains the same no matter how few his / her teaching hours may become in a pay period. It also means that the unused teaching hours of one pay period can't be moved for use in next pay period/s.

Teaching hours are organized by the school, in a block, a maximum of ___ hours (___ or ___ minute class, ___ minutes break) a day, from Monday through Friday from ___ hrs. to ___ hrs, daily.

The employee will participate 'on his/her time', in a maximum of 3 school events, each no longer than 7 hours, in one contract year. A 5-minutes preparation time for each class session, and a 30-minutes teachers' meeting per week is also 'on employee's time'.

** Unpaid class preparation is a maximum of 5 minutes, before each class. More than that will be considered as overtime.

**Overtime is not obligatory. Any activity for or with the school in excess of what is agreed upon here (in paragraph 2), will be regarded as overtime.

> ** Good schools will not keep you at school longer than 6 or 7 continuous hours a day. Split shifts and longer shifts do waste your morning and evening together. If the total of 4 or 5 hours a day are organized in two blocks during the day in a way that it gives you plenty of time to enjoy your days/nights, it may be a good choice to take the job provided the hours are written in the contract. This is important so that directors cannot increase or spread them later in the year. Some hagwons will offer you a contract with hours from 3 PM to 9 PM, 5 days a week; and after*

a couple of months, try to give you a split-shift. That's why the hours of presence at the school must be in the contract.

3. PERIOD OF EMPLOYMENT

The total Agreement term is ___ calendar months, from ___ / ___ / 2004, to ___ / ___ / ___

5. SALARY & OVERTIME PAYMENT

a. The period of four continuous weeks, or one month, is one 'Pay Period'. There can be no unpaid gaps in one pay period, and there can be no unpaid gaps between two pay periods, from the first day to the last day of this contract.

b. Regardless of how few the employee's work hours in a 'pay period' may be, his/her minimum pay is (A): ___Won per 4 weeks (28 continuous days) or per one month. All vacations, national holidays and maximum 6 annual leave/sick-days are also paid at the same rate without the employee being asked to work to make up for these days.

> *For an inexperienced person with a BA degree, the salary should not be lower than two million won for one-hundred guaranteed hours in 4 weeks. Some school contracts say one-hundred hours in one month, while mentioning twenty-five hour work weeks. Sometimes, that creates an unpaid gap of 2 to 3 days a month (some months are more than four weeks). I think you're just out of luck on this one. The monthly pay is the monthly pay, no matter how many days in each month there are. I just consider those unpaid extra days each month as justification for all of my paid vacations, holidays, and sick time!*

c. Overtime. Any action and participation of the employee at the school or outside, directed by the school, that is above the agreed upon hours mentioned in this contract, is regarded as overtime work and is compensated with (B)___ Won / 60 minutes.

d. Overtime is calculated and paid on Monthly Basis together with the monthly pay. Work / service hours in excess of 100 hours a month *(or whatever your maximum hours per month are)*, is considered as overtime work. Overtime includes any of the following done outside of work hours: Extra class-preparation and making teaching material at the school *(if requested by the director)*, translating, on the clock meetings, open house, entertaining parents, student minding after working hours are over, extra-curricular activities, *and any other action or participation in or outside school that is arranged in agreement between the teacher and the director.

> *Be aware that some schools try to keep the overtime pay until the end of the contract, and on the way, find excuses to avoid paying it to you. Honest schools pay the overtime with your salary every month. Be sure that your contract is clear that overtime is to be paid on a monthly basis.*

e. The monthly pay of the employee will be made without delay on or prior to the 'pay day' that is the___day of each month. The payment of the salary and overtime are made up to date on the pay day. If the pay day falls on a holiday, the payment will be made on the last workday before.

The payment of the last month's salary and overtime, plus the annual bonus will be made on the employee's last workday.

f. If the school requires the teacher to travel to different workplaces, all hours of traveling/work in excess of ___ working, and ___ traveling hours a week will be considered as work hours, and the school will also pay for the full cost of the employee's traveling from his/her home, to all the workplaces, and back to his/her home.

> *Schools that require you to travel long distances in excess of your teaching hours at their school can be troubling and annoying. I have heard of teachers having to take several modes of transportation; bus, subway, taxi, just to get to school everyday. Your accommodations and your school shouldn't be more than walking distance or a short bus ride away.*

6. TAX & DEDUCTIBLES

Income tax of 3.5%, and the employee's half of the 'health insurance premium' of ___ Won will be deducted from the employee's monthly pay. No other fees whatsoever will be deducted from the employee's pay unless agreed upon in advance.

> *Other fees can include national pension program (you may be able to opt out of this if you want) and various utility and phone bills the teacher may be responsible for.*

An absolutely necessary point: at the time of this writing, income tax is approximately 3.5%. Half of the health insurance premium you are required to pay should not be more than forty-thousand to fifty-thousand won per month. The school (not you) should pay your immigration, visa, and foreign identification card fees.

7. RENT FREE, FURNISHED HOUSING

Housing is a rent-free, private (not shared) flat in a house or in an apartment building. The flat is Clean & Quiet. The flat includes a bedroom, kitchenette / living room, a bathroom, etc.

Basements, shared flats, dark, humid, dirty, or rat / mold -infested places, or places in noisy or dangerous areas are not considered as acceptable accommodations.

The clean rent-free apartment will be offered to the employee on his/her arrival day, and it must be returned to the school in the same shape when the employee leaves the institute.

Furniture should be in clean and good (not worn-out) condition. Bed, bedding, sheets, desk, curtains, closet, table, dining set, VCR, TV, washing machine, phone, fridge, stove, clothes rack, pots, pans, dishes, cutlery, fan or air conditioning, and a working heating system, are already in the apartment.

The furniture and the appliances provided are clean and in good working condition, and must be returned to the school in the same condition on the last day of this contract.

Maintenance of, and Repairs to the apartment, the appliances, and the heating system, as well as replacement of worn-out furniture, are the responsibility of the employer.

The utilities must be paid by the employee on monthly basis.

8. SAME DAY RESPONSE

Should the employee report a problem with the heating system, fridge or stove, or should s/he need medical attention, on the same day, the employer will help or hire help to solve the problem.

9. PAID HOLIDAYS, LEAVE & SICK-DAYS

The employee will have one week paid vacation in winter, and another week of paid vacation in the summer. The vacation time is announced to the employee at least 2 months in advance. The paid vacations are in addition to the 6 paid leave / sick days per year. A physician's approval is needed if the employee needs to take more than one sick-day at a time. All these days are paid, meaning the employee is paid the same salary and overtime pay as usual and will not be asked to work extra hours to make up for these days, nor can these days come off his overtime hours. The vacations come in minimum of one-week blocks, and cannot be divided.

10. DRESS CODE

Clean and proper shirts and pants in the winter, Dressy shorts and T-shirts in the summer are acceptable work attire.

> *(this can be modified or written differently depending on your place of work)*

11. MEDICAL INSURANCE

From his first workday the employee will be covered for his dental and medical insurance by the 'Korean National Medical Insurance'. One half of the insurance premium is to be paid by the employer and another half is to be paid by the employee.

Payment of the employee's half of the insurance premium will be made by deduction of the same out of his/her monthly salary. The premium rate is ___ of the monthly pay.

12. AIRFARE, VISA, & 'VISA RUN'

A prepaid economy class round trip ticket is sent to the employee, by the employer, so to fly him/her from the international airport closest to his/her original home address, to his/her workplace in Korea. The employee keeps the return ticket.

> *Sometimes, two separate tickets will be purchased, each one-way. The second ticket may not be purchased for you until completion of your contract. This is normal. Be ready to question schools that offer to reimburse you for tickets. Reputable schools will normally purchase the ticket for you, although, there have been instances that I know of very reputable schools reimbursing airfare.*

Sometimes it's a toss-up.

Should the employer need to send the employee to another country to obtain a Korean work visa, it will be done immediately upon arrival to Korea, and all costs of traveling / transportation, hotel, and food for the visa trip will be covered by the employer.

All costs of residence visa and residence card in Korea are also covered by the employer.

13. BONUSES

In accordance to the Korean labor law, the annual severance equivalent of the employee's monthly pay, is paid to the employee on the last day of this contract REGARDLESS of his/her renewing his/her contract for another year. Six-month contracts should come with a bonus of half a month's salary.

Contract Renewal Bonus of 2/3 of the teacher's salary is paid to him/her upon renewal of this contract for another year. The next year's contract will not offer a round trip airfare. An annual pay raise of 5% will be added for the second year's contract. The conditions of the contract can be renegotiated by the parties for a second year's contract.

The employers in Korea decide on a salary rate while taking to account these standard Korean bonuses. Every Korean and foreign worker in Korea is entitled to these bonuses - the bonuses are actually parts of your annual salary.

14. DISCIPLINING STUDENTS

Due to the employee's lack of knowledge of the students' mother tongue and culture, the school principal and the local assistants will eagerly assist the employee, should s/he ask for help in disciplining the students.

15. DISMISSAL OR VOLUNTARY RESIGNATION

The employer and the employee reserve the right to end this contract, in any of the cases mentioned in this paragraph.

* It is agreed hereby that a copy of the employee's resignation or dismissal notice will act as his/her legal 'Release Paper'.

Dismissal can take place if the employee:

a. neglects his/her duties stipulated in this agreement.
b. is frequently absent from work.
c. does not report to work for over 15 days.
d. has to take an extended (longer than 30 days) sick leave even if recommended by a registered physician.

*In cases 'a' and 'b', the employee will have 20 days after each warning letter, to correct the situation. In case 'c', the employee will be paid to the last day of his/her Work. In case 'd' the employee's last paid day will be the dismissal day.

Resignation can take place if the employee perceives:

a. continuous disrespect, or negligence of his/her human rights.
b. employer's negligence of the points of this contract, including on-time pay.
c. death or severe illness of a family member, or severe illness of the employee.

In case of resignation, employee is paid up to his/her last day of Work, and no fees except for the amount shown on his/her apartment utility bills, plus his/her monthly 'income tax & health insurance premium' - will be deducted from his pay.

All the accounts / salary, as explained in this contract, must be settled by the last day of teacher's work.

The employer will automatically give the 'release paper' to the employee on the last day of this contract. Any further co-operation of the employer and the employee can only happen after the employee has received the release paper.

During the last two months of this contract's period the employer cannot dismiss the employee unless the employer pays the employee his annual bonus, in addition to his up to date pay, on his last workday.

> *(This is to stop illegal dismissal by an employer that wants to save the annual bonus pay by firing an employee).*

A release paper is normally needed even if you fulfill your one year contract. Without it, you may have a difficult time finding work in Korea with another employer.

16. GOVERNING LAW & JURISDICTION

This Agreement is governed by the 'Korean Labor Law for Foreign workers' . As expressed by this Law: at any moment the conditions provided in a work contract must be the same or better than the conditions required by the 'Labor Law'.

This Agreement is made final and firm.

School's Name and address:

Employer's name   Employee's name

Employer's signature   Employee's signature

Date & place of signing

Example of the Second Teaching Contract:

Employer: _____
Hereafter to be referred to as the employer

Employee: _____
Hereafter to be referred to as the employee

The parties agree as follows:
1: TERM OF CONTRACT
This contract will be valid for a period of twelve months beginning _____ and ending _____.

2: CONDITIONS OF EMPLOYMENT
The employee will act in an appropriately professional manner and be responsible for conducting professional English language classes.
The employee will be required to work for regularly scheduled hours from Monday to Friday, each teaching hour in excess of _____ hours a week is considered as overtime. (One hour is sixty minutes)
Classes and teaching hours are scheduled at the institute's sole discretion.
The employee is required to go through an orientation and training program before starting employment.

3: SERVICES PROVIDED BY THE EMPLOYER
Payment and tax: The employer will pay a monthly salary of _____

for regularly scheduled hours which were mentioned previously. (payment of salary commences from the first day of teaching).

The employer may ask the employee to work overtime (the employee has an option to refuse and will not be forced), and if the employee chooses to do overtime, the employer will pay for the overtime at the rate of _____.

The employee salary will be paid at the end of each month.

Tax, pension for income will be deducted from the salary according to the Korean tax law, and the employer will provide the employee with the receipt for this.

4: HOUSING

The employer will provide the employee a furnished _____ and the housing will be provided at no cost to the employee with the exception of maintenance and phone bills (and utilities). A two-person apartment/house will be provided for a couple if both are teaching at the institute.

5: AIRFARE

Employer shall provide round-trip ticket. In the event that employee willfully leaves the employer before his/her contract, employer is not responsible for the return airfare. If employee willfully leaves the employer before six months, employee must pay back the initial airfare and employer may deduct the said airfare from employee's last pay.

6: MEDICAL INSURANCE

Half of the insurance premium will be paid by the employee and the other half by the employer.

7: SEVERANCE PAY

Upon completion of this contract, the employer will pay one month's salary as a severance payment to the employee. This payment will be made at the time of completion of the contract period.

8: VACATION

The employee may have ten working days as paid vacation as well as all Korean national holidays per year, which will be organized by the institute. (Days in which the employee does not regularly work, i.e. Saturdays, Sundays, and national holidays are not to be considered as part of the vacation period). Employee's paid sick leave during the term of employment shall not exceed three calendar days. (A doctor's invoice with the diagnosis and prognosis is required to be paid for sick days).

9: RENEWAL AND TERMINATION OF CONTRACT

Renewal: The employee must give the employer a written sixty-day notice before renewal or non-renewal of the employee's current contract.
Both the employer and the employee reserve the option to renew the contract.
Termination of contract: Both parties will give at least a written sixty-day notice prior to the termination date of the contract.
The employer retains the right to terminate the contract immediately if:
The employee is unable to discharge the Responsibilities or meet the conditions such as being late for class on a continuous basis, continuous failure to keep regularly scheduled class hours, and repeated absences from classes without a valid reason.
Employee teaches a private class outside school.
Employee participates in any type of criminal Activity or corruption of public morals which violates the laws of the Republic of South Korea.

If, for any reason, the contract is terminated before the full completion of the contract period: 1) the employee will not qualify for benefits such as severance pay and airfaire.
2) the employee will be wholly responsible for any maintenance and phone bills remaining for the duration of the housing lease.

Within fourteen days the employee is required to sign a notice of termination and accompany the employer to the Korean Immigration office to notify the Korean immigration office of the termination.

10: GOVERNING LAW AND JURISDICTION
This contract is governed by the law of the Republic of Korea.
This contract is made final and firm unless any material modification or amendment to this contract is executed with the full knowledge and consent of the undersigned and incorporated into this contract.

In witness thereof, we have affixed our signatures hereon.
Date:_____

_____
Employer signature

_____
Employee signature

(Employee's schedule to be listed here).

Chapter 8:

Conversations

The following are conversations I have had with some English teachers teaching in Korea. The situations are real but I have changed the names to protect their anonymity. These glimpses into their experiences are valuable in that they tell you what you can expect at different institutions and in different community settings. Take note of how they have been able to cope with situations and what their cultural and professional opinions of Korea are. These opinions can help you decide if living and working in Korea is right for you.

August 4th, 2005. Howard from Australia

Introduce yourself. What are you doing here in South Korea?

I'm on the wrong side of fifty, and I came to Korea primarily to alleviate boredom. I was hoping that I may rediscover some creativity again—and it's working. I'm back practicing at least one hour of music everyday. I brought my flute with me and someone's loaning me his guitar. So, I could bring my flute with me because it doesn't weigh much. So yes. Having been to Korea before I knew more of what I wanted to do here, and that was to teach adults. I did not want to have anything to do with young children. So, I spent time just looking for a hagwon for adults only. Out of three applications I put in, UES (United English School) was the one that called me.

How long were you searching for a job in South Korea?

Well, not long. Maybe about a week or a week and a half. No, it didn't even take me that long. It was just a matter of days. It took me about a week and a half to get a lot of my things together, like my documentations ready.

How many years ago was it when you first came to South Korea to teach English?

It was in 2000 to 2001. I was in Jungpei, which is in Kangwon province for about thirteen months. I worked at a very good hagwon. The people I worked for were very nice and honorable. So, I had a very good hagwon experience. The funny thing was, I was a little dissatisfied with some things for the first three months, but then I met some of the other expatriates and I saw what they were putting up with, and then I realized that I was working for the best hagwon in town. We had air-conditioned classrooms and I had a computer at my disposal, and photocopiers and VCR's. I had everything I wanted. But, I knew a lot of Koreans at the time, some of whom visited Australia. Some of them had even stayed with me. Yes, my experience so far has been very nice. I find that Koreans are very easy to get to know, very easy to make friends with.

Why did you stay for a little over a year? Was your original contract more than twelve months?

No, they asked me to stick around until they found a new teacher.

I see. Of course, they probably waited until the last minute to find somebody.

Yes, they did. You know how it works here. And then everything is "Bali, bali!" (Quickly, quickly in Korean).

How did you feel when you first decided to take the job at UES?

I made up my mind that I was coming back to Korea, so, it was just a matter of finding what looked to be a suitable position. I guess I can say that I knew what I was coming back to. I'm quite comfortable with the job. There are problems with language here, of course, but that's part of the adventure. If you're gonna worry about not having language, you can make yourself sick worrying about just day to day living, and then, why come. But, it's not a problem. The little problems I do have, what can I say, they're not really problems. You can always overcome them somehow. If you think of your own country, think about people in your own country, then think about the people here in South Korea who are bigoted. The bigoted people are always the less intelligent people who are going to always say, "Oh, why don't they speak English (or Korean)!" Or, "those bloody foreigners," you understand? You may get a taxi driver or something with this mentality. On the other side of the coin, you get some really nice taxi drivers who will understand you.

When you first started working at UES, how did you feel? Did you feel like you fell into a good situation with taking this job?

Well, there's no interference in what you do, that's the really good thing. As long as you're doing your job okay, they won't (Korean management) interfere. Now, the management, over some issue, often will not bend. However, I have learned that I can use other things as leverage. Like, if maybe you're required to attend a meeting or something, and I just won't go to meetings. Then, I just wait until they come to me, and then I just say, "Okay, this is how we're going to compromise. You do this for me, and I'll go to the meeting for you." I find that it works.

Do you feel like you're respected by your Korean superiors?

That doesn't bother me. I don't care what they think about me, because, um, this is going to sound like a burst of arrogance but I don't mean it this way. I know that I have the intellectual authority. So, it doesn't matter what they think of me, because that's not important. Just as long as the pay is in my bank account at the end of each month.

Do you create your own curriculum?

They have a curriculum supplied. They produce a lot of things in-house. They produce their own textbooks. That's a mixed quality. Sometimes there are good things in those books, and I'm happy to use them, but other times there are quite boring materials. I just put my own material and resources in. It's not an issue. If I don't like what's on the schedule that day, I don't bother with it. I have a lot of teaching freedom and I wouldn't expect it to be any other way.

Does the Korean staff at your school get along well with the foreign staff? Are there any communication or cultural barriers?

I don't think so. They often go out to lunch together. Often times the expats (we all live in the same building), maybe once or twice a month, will put on a barbecue. The Korean staff comes too.

How about any conflict between the Korean superiors (the boss) and the foreign staff?

I'm sure there is some miscommunication sometimes. Good question. I haven't seen very much. I haven't seen any major conflicts. It may be happening and I just don't know.

What differences do you see, overall, between Korean people and foreigners here in South Korea?

That's a very subjective question. I think what surprises me, and it shouldn't surprise me, because I saw it in Jungpei. Nevertheless, I was surprised by it all the time. The expatriates that live here (in South Korea) keep themselves segregated from the local people, you know what I mean? You know, there's a lot of men I've met here that have Korean girlfriends, but that doesn't mean that they're bridging any cultural gaps or any social gaps. That's just that they happened to acquire, you know, an attractive partner.

So you're saying that the Korean people and the foreigners pretty much keep themselves segregated.

Yes, I think so. Or at least that's how it seems to me. Um, people may tell you things differently, 'cause I mean, you know, not withstanding the fact that they go out together for lunch sometimes. But, to what extent they try to blend in with the locals, I don't know, it's my own interpretation that they just don't. Once again, you may be asking the wrong person. My view may be a bit different than others. The thing I keep hearing expats say is that they're only going to be here (in South Korea) for a short time, maybe for a year. But friendships can last longer than that year. There are people that I've met in Jungpei five years ago that I still communicate with, by email or by telephone.

Do you think that Koreans and expats keep themselves segregated because there is some kind of culture clash, or they don't fully understand how to behave with this person?

Oh yes, yes. I've also had Koreans say to me that they will avoid the 'weigook' (foreigner) because, for a number of reasons. Sometimes they feel a little bit insecure. Sometimes because they (the Koreans) feel, just out of politeness, that they don't want to impose their broken English on them (the foreigners). That's what they say most of the time. That's what they'll tell you. But other times, the same people have told me that the reason they don't like foreigners is because the foreigners are haughty. That word 'haughty' came up on many, many occasions.

What does that mean?

Sort of arrogant. And that word 'haughty' comes up often.

Do you think they (Koreans) have a point?

Perhaps. I mean, it only takes one foreigner to act like that, and then everyone knows about it and every foreigner in the district becomes that way, in the Korean's eyes.

What were some of your best moments in Korea?

Some of my best moments? I've probably had many best moments, maybe they've been, you know, small moments, but they were some very good moments. There have been times when someone has just spontaneously invited me to join their party. And, there I am with no Korean skills, and there they are with no English skills, but yet we're drinking together. We'd laugh at each other's body language and nonverbal communication. Moments like that are quite special. I haven't really had any 'sightseeing moments' or anything. I had a really, really nice four days in Seoul one time. I stayed with a Korean family. That was really, really nice. It was the first snow of the season in Seoul. Yeah, there was a lot of things special about those four days. We ate very well too. That Korean family took me to many places.

Did you have any worst moments in Korea?

Not really, not really. There were some stressful times, but looking back on it, if I had approached those situations differently I would not have allowed myself to stress over them. But, you have to get out and get on with it.

July 19th, 2005. Doug from the United States.

Introduce yourself. Who are you, how old are you, and what do you do here in Korea?

I'm Doug French, I'm 26 years old, and I teach English illegally in Korea.

How long have you been doing this for?

Since November, so I guess for nine months.

Why do you say you're teaching illegally?

Because I'm here on a tourist visa working at a job that requires a working visa.

So, do you teach at a school?

I teach for a small business that offers private lessons and contracts me out to hagwons or kindergartens.

That's exclusively what you do?

Yes

Was this the job you originally had when you first came to Korea?

No. My first job I was teaching at a hagwon for a month. But I couldn't get the working visa so I had to leave. After I left I found this current job.

How did you first feel when you decided to come to Korea and teach?

Uh, yeah. I was excited to come out here and try something new. I knew that I didn't have really desirable qualifications as a teacher, so perhaps I was concerned about my own ability to import knowledge to my students. I knew that there were a lot of people working out here that didn't necessarily have great qualifications, so, I wasn't really worried about that.

Why did you originally decide to come to Korea to work?

Um, it was a combination of several factors. I had a girlfriend at the time that came out here first and she said that she was doing very well. So, I thought that it would be a good idea not only to be with her but also to make money. At the time I was falling behind in my finances and I saw this as a chance to catch up. I think also, a big reason why I came out here was to travel and see more of the world and to have an opportunity to experience Asia firsthand.

How did you feel when you started working for the first job (the hagwon)?

How did I feel?

Yes. Did you feel like it was going to work out? Did you feel "iffy" about the situation? How did you feel?

Yeah, I felt that I was a pretty good teacher, actually. I was enjoying teaching. I liked the kids and I liked the people I was working with. So, yeah, I guess I was optimistic about it.

You switched to the second job after you couldn't get the working visa for the first job. Why did you apply specifically for your current job?

This job advertised publicly that they could employ you as a teacher and that a bachelor's degree was not required. A bachelor's degree is required to obtain the E2 visa (the visa that you need to teach English in Korea). So, I thought that perhaps this company was exploiting some loophole in the law. I discovered that they were basically just bribing immigration. That was good enough for me.

Are you happy with the job that you have now?

I have mixed feelings about the job that I have now. The pay is not as good as some of the legitimate jobs. In certain ways I feel like I haven't been taken care of. But, overall, I'm not really unhappy. I don't feel that there's malicious intent in the way that I have not been taken care of. But uh, just inexperience.

Inexperience?

On the part of my boss.

What kind of person do you think comes to Korea to teach?

Depraved people. Nawww, um, I think generally they are politically liberal people. Generally they are young, but not always. I think that they are people who, like me, want to experience more of the world, who want to travel and don't necessarily have the money to do that on their own. There tend to be sort of fringe elements I think. People who maybe didn't fit in where they came from.

Tell me about the Korean people that you've met.

I find most Korean people that I've met to be friendly and often helpful. I think that to Koreans, foreigners are somewhat of a novelty. We're looked upon as, maybe, sort of a local celebrity status almost. Young children will say "hello" to us when they see us on the street. People will giggle and be embarrassed when we approach them—even if we speak a little Korean. So, like I said, I think that we enjoy sort of a semi-celebrity status here. But I think most people are eager to help us. It does seem difficult to forage really meaningful relationships, although it is possible between foreigners and Koreans. I think that that's a matter of a language barrier more than any real cultural difference. Also, of course, there's the fact that most of us foreigners are not here permanently. We come here and spend a year or two, or three, teaching and then we leave.

*And what significance does that have?

Well, it's difficult for the Koreans to become truly attached to us knowing that we'll probably move on in a matter of months.

*What differences do you see between Koreans and Westerners?

Of course there's a myriad of cultural differences. But most of them are pretty superficial, I think. Speaking purely from my own experience of Westerners, I think that Korean culture is more accepting of minor breaches in trust. If someone is late for an arrangement or an appointment, it matters less here. Appointments, like our lessons, can be cancelled on a very short notice with apparently no ill feelings between the Koreans. Officials can be easily bribed, it seems, on minor matters, like immigration work. These things are considered a bigger deal where I come from. (Where I come from) People might accept your tardiness once, but probably not twice. Certainly officials are expected not to take bribes. (In the West) This is much less expected and much more difficult it seems like.

*Do you think teaching English in Korea, immigration, and Korean employers are somewhat corrupt?

Yes. I think that there's a deep vain of corruption that runs through this industry, in these groups of hagwons and English lesson providers, as well as the Korean government. I think that there's sort of an expectation that Korean employers will be able to take advantage of their employees to some minor degree. And this may not just be with English teachers; this may be universal to Korean employment. It seems that Korean employees do not question their superiors in the same way that we do in the West. For example, I had a friend, a Korean friend, who worked for a company for three months. During these three months, his rate of pay had not yet been settled upon and he was not being paid. So, he essentially worked without pay for three months, at the end of which, his employer decided that he wasn't going to pay him at all. And so he left, having put in three months for this company. He left without receiving any pay at all. Clearly, this would have been wildly unacceptable in the West, and at the very least would involve some form of litigation. Certainly, not everyone would blame him for just going through the business place and shooting people.

What did your friend do when he left the company without getting paid?

That's just it. He left the company without getting paid. That's exactly what he did. He got another job.

What do you think about this?

It's not what I would have done (leaving the company without getting paid). I think he was foolish for doing so. I would have started by raising a lot of hell about it.

Has that ever happened to you while working in Korea?

Certainly not. No. I have, on occasion, had my employers try to take advantage of me. Both of my employers (the fist and the second) have taken more taxes than they should have. My first legitimate employer took about five percent tax out of my wage, which really she should have taken, at most, 3.6%. And then, of course, my current employer employs me illegally and does not pay tax on my wage. But he chose to take tax out of my wage anyway.

Do you know why?

Yes. He wanted to keep the money. The business that he runs is part of a franchise, and he has periodic meetings with the other franchise owners. This is common practice among them. He adopted it (taxing his workers' wages) merely as common practice, it seems. Of course, when I confronted him about it he paid me back the money and he hasn't taken taxes out since.

Do you feel that there is a culture clash between Koreans and Westerners here in Korea, or Koreans and foreign staff at any of your jobs? If so, in what way?

Culture Clash. Yeah. But generally not with me. For example, at my current place of employment there's another instructor who often feels that she's having culture clashes with the boss. She expects him to give her adequate notice before cancelling a class, expects him to give her more documentation than he actually gives, expects him to take care of matters dealing with her apartment, etc. etc. But, uh, he fails to do these things frequently. Now, whether this is a real culture clash or just an issue with this particular, perhaps not entirely mature gentleman, it's difficult to say. But, I'm assuming that it's sort of a culture clash related to my earlier point about Koreans seeming to accept breaches of trust that Westerners would not accept as easily. Personally, however, I don't seem to really experience culture shock, and culture clashes go along with that. I just accept the way that things are. So, I don't have a lot of culture clashes.

Why do you think some Westerners that work here, including your coworker, have these culture clashes with their Korean bosses and their Korean counterparts?

Is this a trick question? The easiest answer is because they come from a different culture and they have different expectations and human relationships.

What were some of your best moments working in Korea so far?

You have certain lessons that just go off very well. You have certain students that you look forward to teaching. I don't know that any episodes specially stand out in my mind, but I certainly have students that I look forward to seeing.

Have there ever been any special moments not related to your job, such as travelling to certain parts of the country or seeing something in particular?

Sure. Every time I go somewhere and experience something new it's exciting for me. So, for example, when I went to Gyeryoungsan, which is a national park, it was fun for me to see the old temples and to climb the mountains. It was rather beautiful. When I went to Seoul, it was exciting. That's a big bustling city. There were so many people and so many different things to see. I also went to Busan and took a boat to Japan. I suppose we're leaving Korea at that point, but the whole trip was really pretty marvelous. I think one of my favorite things about Korea is its proximity to the rest of Asia. It's easy to travel from here and easy to go to other places. I took a vacation to Thailand and to Malaysia. I've been to Japan. And I'm certainly not the most travelled of my peers. So, it's a pretty good opportunity for that.

How about the DMZ? Did you see that?

I did. I went up to the DMZ. It certainly was moving. The separation of Korea is almost a dominating landmark of the Korean psychological landscape. It's amazing how much this division affects them on a daily basis fifty years after—or, in fact even more than that—sixty years after their separation.

Certainly I would have expected them to have basically adapted, not to think about it very often anymore. But that's not the case. I frequently talk to Koreans about their separation and they tell me how they pray and hope for reunification with North Korea. So yeah, the DMZ is the focus of a lot of pathos here in Korea.

*What were some of your worst moments working in Korea?

Oh, you know. You get kids that throw tantrums, and their parents coddle them. That's the same as teaching anywhere, I'm sure. Worst moments? I don't like Kindergartens. I have to teach Kindergartens now and them, and it's very difficult for a Westerner to control them. They see us generally once a week. We're sort of a novelty, a funny character almost that comes in and does a little bit for twenty or thirty minutes. It's very difficult with limited Korean and limited contact with these children to control them. Basically, if the Korean kindergarten teacher does not make an effort to help us keep the kids under control, a lot of the impact of the lesson is really lost. Sometimes, I reflect that these schools who call upon my boss to provide an English teacher for an hour a week, or however long, really just want to have some exposure for their children to Western people. I don't know how much English we actually teach. I think that perhaps hagwon owners, or kindergarten owners, can charge more for their service if they can claim that they expose children to us—to native English speakers.

*How do you feel about being considered a novelty?

Um. It beats not being considered. I don't know. It's fine. It doesn't bother me.

*Do you think it bothers some teachers who are trying to make a difference?

Sure. Well, I think this about all teachers. Everybody comes in full of fire, trying to make a difference. Eventually, the fire burns out, and you just get through the day. And it's just a job.

*Do you feel that you've been treated fairly in Korea and at your job in particular?

Yeah, fundamentally. I don't really think Koreans generally discriminate against me. It seems that they try to help me, and often go out of their way to help me. On the job, I think that in the beginning maybe my boss tried to take advantage of me. It's hard to say for sure. But I don't think he does that anymore. I think that maybe he discovered that it didn't work. He discovered that I'm not as dumb as I look.

What kinds of things have you been unhappy with at your current job?

Well, I don't think that the boss does as much for me as he could to make me comfortable and happy. For example, he provides me with a one-room apartment, but now this one-room apartment is infested with insects and he has not taken any steps to help me with alleviating this insect infestation. Not knowing Korean, it would be very difficult for me to obtain that kind of help on my own, besides which I don't think I should have to pay for it. But overall, I'm not unhappy with how I'm treated. I think I'm treated fairly well, all things considered.

What kinds of things have you been happy with at your current job or in Korea in general?

You know, for me it's all about the people. You meet some people who are very kind and very friendly or are just somehow compatible with you, just like living anywhere. I have students and friends who have made me happy. I've enjoyed meeting people from other countries, which is not as common in the United States. There it's difficult to get a visa, you know, if you don't live in the United States it's difficult to visit. So, it's given me the opportunity to meet a lot of people that I would not have otherwise been able to meet. I'm learning Korean. That makes me happy. It gives me a sense of accomplishment. Koreans themselves seem fairly impressed when I can speak a few lines of Korean. Some of the food is excellent.

If you had to do it all over again, what would you have changed?

Not much. I might have negotiated my contract a little differently. I probably would have stipulated that I didn't want to teach kindergartens. But not a lot. I'm pretty happy with my experience here and I think that it has benefitted me.

In what way has it benefitted you?

First of all, virtually my entire income here is disposable. I don't have to pay for room and board, the cost of living in Korea is very low, so I've been able to pay off all my debts and generally get back on top of my finances. It's given me further impetus for self-improvement. I'm considering getting more education and coming back to Korea to teach at a University—legally, someday.

What do you miss about your home country?

Well, primarily I miss the people that I was close to in my home country—my friends. I miss Mexican food. I miss driving. Not that I couldn't drive here, but I don't have a car. I miss chairs. I guess that's it. I think I've adapted pretty well here.

What will you miss about Korea after you leave?

I'll be heading back to California where the cost of living is very high, and I think that it will be a shock to me when I go into a store, or when I go to pay my rent, exactly how much that actually costs. But yeah, not much.

Will you be missing Korean food?

Probably not. That's just not my makeup. I'll get back and I'll be enjoying my Mexican food and hamburgers, or whatever the heck I'm eating. I won't really miss what I'm not eating.

Tell me about what the typical English teaching contract looks like.

The typical contract, at the moment, pays about two million Won per month, provides room and board which is generally a one-room apartment—pretty small. I'm sorry, it does not provide board. It provides the room, lodging, which is the one-room apartment with a small bed, usually a T.V; a kitchenette arrangement, which is usually a part of the one room; a small bathroom that has a spigot on the wall to shower with. The contract provides two weeks vacation which is separated to a one week vacation and another one week vacation later on. It also pays travel expenses to and from the home country for the one time. Once to come out to Korea and once to go back to their home country, assuming that the contract is completed. The contract often provides a one-month severance pay at the end of the contract. That's a typical hagwon contract.

Will you be staying at your current job for awhile?

No. I'm leaving in about five weeks. Sorry, six weeks.

Why?

I want to go back to school. The time that I'll be leaving this job coincides with the beginning of the school year back in America. I'm gonna go back to America and go back to school so that I can come back out to Korea and work legally as soon as possible. Or I may not come back to Korea, but it's an option. The ratio of the cost of living to the wages paid is very good in Korea.

On a scale of one to ten, ten being the most difficult, what would you say is the degree of difficulty getting around in Korea, not knowing the language?

Just getting around I would say is pretty low. Maybe a four or a five. The buses are a little bit difficult because the bus destinations on the signs are all written in Korean. But, if you go to Seoul, the subway system is easily navigated. People generally speak enough English that you can get by, and you can use just a little bit of pigeon Korean to get by. It's certainly a hell of a lot easier than Japan, which is a big, huge pain in my ass. But, to get specific things done, things that tourists or foreigners don't often need to get done, can be difficult. For example, at one point I was looking for a piece of insulation foam. It was very, very difficult to describe that to people who generally don't know what that is. They don't know where to look for that. So, yeah, specific tasks are often more difficult. But, I'd say, just to live here—to get groceries, to go to the movies, you know, whatever you want to do on a daily basis is actually very easy.

What kind of advice would you give people who are thinking about coming to Korea to teach English?

I don't recommend doing what I've done and teaching illegally. It is somewhat stressful. It's not the way to go, and I make less money than the other hagwon teachers. And I have to work just as much to make anywhere near what they make a month. If you can do it, get a university job, that's the way to go, that's the Cadillac of jobs around here. The universities have something on the line, and as a result, I think that they're less ready to take advantage of you, less ready to smear their name by some short-sighted tactic. However, if you don't have a master's degree it may be more difficult to get a university job. So, you can take a hagwon job or what have you. If you're not the kind of person who really likes little, tiny children, don't teach kindergartens because it's very, very difficult to control kindergarteners if you don't speak Korean. They don't recognize you as an authority figure. But overall, I recommend the entire experience. I think it's a good way to go and I think that a lot of people can benefit from it in more ways than one.

November 10, 2008. Nate Chang from Canada.

What kind of school do you teach at? How long have you taught there?

I teach at Jincheon Girls Middle School, Baekgok Middle School and Jincheon high school.

What do you teach?

I am a support teacher for each of the grades. I encourage the learning of English at the schools.

How has your experience been, working in a rural elementary school and high school?

Working in rural middle school is very peaceful. I am often used to the city life where there is always something happening, but the country life has been very nice. Working in a small town you get to see your students on the street more often. It is a great way to interact with students outside of class.

What are your co-teachers and contact people like?

My contact people have always been good. I try not to apply any pressure. I know things take a while to get done. Usually, if you are patient, things get done quicker. It's a great working relationship, especially if you can develop dialogue with your contact people or co-teachers.

How is the office environment and social environment? Are they organized?

The working environment is very friendly. Co-teachers always encourage me to participate in sports activities. The teachers are usually pretty organized but as the foreigner, I am usually the last to know about class changes. But that also has to do with not know the scheduling program on the computers.

Are there any communication difficulties?

There are always communication difficulties. As long as both sides do their best that is all we can hope for. But since we are people outside of Korean culture, it's best that we give more of an effort because Korean is the native tongue here. So, learning a bit (of the language) helps.

How are the attitudes of the students?

The attitudes of the students vary; some really want to learn English. Others don't. They are young and they don't quite value the skills teachers try and teach them. There are future benefits, but they are young and don't see that far ahead yet.

How do you feel about the English education system here in Korea? What do you think should be changed?

The English education system is in a state of flux. I think there does need to be changes made, but it's also hard for public systems to compete with the private ones and still expect a balanced system for everyone. Though, I would like see more balance between speaking, listening, reading, and writing. I personally believe writing is a great way to develop speaking skills. Changes to the system take time and patience.

What kind of person do you think comes to Korea to teach?

I don't know. That's difficult to answer.

As a Canadian, do you feel you're treated well by the staff at your school?

It's hard to say, because I am Chinese Canadian and so most Koreans do not see me as a typical Canadian. On the whole, I find people very friendly in Jincheon. If you make a few key friends here and there the teaching experience feels a lot more rewarding. The staff at the schools is amazing. Always friendly and cheerful, in spite of the language barriers, it is important for both sides to try.

February 25, 2005. Rob Williams from the United States.

*Who are you?

My name is Rob Williams, I am 48 years old, and I teach at Kids College Kindergarten and Elementary school for English. I'm an English teacher for kindergarten and elementary.

*How long have you been doing that?

As of March first, one year, I'm almost done. Time to go home.

*How did you first feel when you first decided to take the job in Korea? How did you feel when you accepted the job?

Scared to death, desperate, not sure. There were so many thoughts going through my head. I didn't have the money to do anything in California, I moved back to Wisconsin. The school in Korea wasn't sure they wanted me because they said I was too old. But I had no idea what I was doing. I had my certificate to teach English, but, I didn't know Korea, and I just said, well, I gotta make a decision today—yes or no. So, I decided to go. I didn't really have a lot of time to think about it, and they needed a teacher within a week. I had like, three days to pack and get ready to go. I didn't think, I just said, "Okay, do it," and I took off.

Did you read the employment contract?

Yeah, I read it. It seemed okay. But I had also seen stuff on the internet that said to be careful with contracts and Korean businesspeople and all that, but I wasn't in a position—I saw two million won a month, and I said "okay, okay," and my only goal was to save as much money as I could. I knew I would have to put up with some bullshit because I've put up with bullshit from every boss I've ever had. So I planned on just saving my money, focus, get my money, turn around, and go home. So, I kind of laugh about it now because I wrote on my contract *Is it possible to extend my contract two or three years*? Oh, dear God I'm glad I didn't do that! So, yeah, I didn't have time to think and I only had one purpose—to save my money—and I reached my goal. My goal was $15,000, and I figured it out last night, I have about $18,000. I'm ahead of the game, so I did what I had to do and I'm ready to go home.

How did you feel when you first started working for the school?

I was excited and nervous, and of course, like when you work at any company, it's "welcome to our family," and two weeks later you say, "Well Christ, I wish I was an orphan." But, Jay (the boss) was all friendly and smiles, and welcoming. He came over to the apartment the night I moved in. He came over on a Saturday and I needed to be at the school on Sunday to go over things a little bit. But he brought me a little peanut sandwich and a little carton of milk. He was all smiley and wonderful, and then it started to unravel gradually. What do they say? Beware of the smile behind the mask? It started to unravel about three weeks into it. But overall, I was excited, I was scared to death, I had never taught little kids before, I had no idea. I became more frightened, because when I signed the contract it said 'English teacher', and then when I got to the airport, John, Jay's assistant, says, "Oh Rob, computers and music class, and arts and crafts!" and I said, "What?! I didn't sign up for this." But, well, too late! So I said, "Okay, I'll do the best I can," and that's all I've been able to do—the best I can. Apparently, it worked out okay.

Well, I know that in the beginning, when you first came to the school, it just opened. There was an opening ceremony. So, everything was new and nobody knew what they were doing. Nobody knew what was going on. You came on the weekend and then right after that you went to the opening ceremony. What was that like?

Um, all the parents were there. And as usual, we weren't told anything. I was under the impression that we would have opening ceremony and then take the afternoon off. Take your breath, and, we'll come back tomorrow and start. So I had to give a little talk to the audience at opening ceremony. I had to introduce myself and tell them a little bit about my background and put their minds at ease. So I got up with my little suit and tie and all that, and gave my bullshit shuffle, and got through it. And then I thought, Oh good, it's over, it's finished, time to go home. Wrong! I had seven little kids sitting in the classroom with presents on their desks! And they said, "Rob, in here?" I said, "But we're going home." And they said, "Oh no. You're gonna start teaching." So, I walked into the room and the teacher's assistant had all these packages. I said, "What am I supposed to do?" All the parents were looking in the window, like "Oh geese, their in good hands." What was I supposed to do? And she said, "Pass these out." So I said to the students, "Okay, welcome to Kid's College, here are your presents, and….welcome." I had no clue what their level was or anything. So I stepped in more deep shit. I went up to the alphabet and I said, "Okay, um, I don't know how much you know, so let's start with the alphabet. "A…." and the kids started going "B,C,D,E,F,G…." And I said to myself, "Oh no! I've got forty minutes to do a whole class!" And I had nothing prepared. Absolutely zero! Oh my God, what was I to do? But like I said, I 'm pretty good with the bullshit shuffle so I just got through the whole day that way. I went home and tried to get something organized. But as you experienced, we're not told anything in advance; nothing—zero. Yeah, it was a hectic first day. I really had no idea what I was doing.

*Did you know the school was just being opened before you took the job?

Yeah, absolutely. Because they contacted me twice in one day. They said, "We'll give you one more chance, do you want to come?" I guess I was there second choice. There was a guy in Seoul that dropped out at the last second. They really didn't want to hire me because I was an old man of 48 and they didn't think I could handle little kids. They thought I'd be too old for them, or whatever nonsense they came up with. But anyways, I knew it was a brand new school and that's what kind of attracted me to it. I thought, *Oh good, I could be one of the first teachers there*, and you know, there's a first time for everything. So, I went over there and I did the best I could. When they finally selected me I said, "Okay let's do it. I'll give it my best shot." And that's all I've ever done. As a matter of fact, as I look back on this year, I don't know if I was a good teacher, but I know every night when I went to bed I thought that maybe things could have gone a bit differently. But I never went to bed thinking that I could have tried harder. Everyday I gave it one-hundred percent. But back to your original question, yes, I kind of liked the fact that the school was new, that way I couldn't get bogged down into their little 'system', hearing them tell me "Well, you have to do it *this* way."

*What kind of person do you think comes to Korea to teach?

There are two kinds of people. There's the one that's just traveling from place to place. Then there are people like you and I, who are desperate. Our backs are to the wall, we can't find a job, and we can't find money. So, I read somewhere that the people who teach English overseas are the ones who are losers in their own country. They can't get it together in their own country so they go overseas and try to make it that way. That's what I heard. I don't know if I read that on the internet somewhere, something about Korea, or what. So, there is that group of people. I was definitely in that group. And then there is that select group that is fascinated with Korea and that Asian culture, and they want to come to Korea to live and work. I came to Korea because the money was pretty good, I mean, at least from what I was told. I didn't know jack about Korea when I got here. All I knew about Korea was the Korean War, what I saw on MASH, and what I saw in the news, "*Riot in Seoul! Film at 11:00!*" You know? And that's all I knew about it. Except, I knew that Korean and Japanese people looked very much alike. And to me, their language sounds a little bit alike. That's all I knew. And, you know, I came here kind of blind, but curious.

*I know that you said that there were jobs in Japan the same like there are in Korea, but the cost of living is high. And in China, the cost of living is low, but you make so little that you can't send the money back home.

Bingo

*So Korea is...

The happy medium. That's exactly right. But, um, I don't know if you have any questions about culture or anything, but, I don't see any culture here in Korea—I mean in Cheonan City. I really don't see it. I see all of these square buildings, and the only Asian architecture I see is that little pavilion at Dankook University, you know, where you go up on that soccer field. But, I mean, everywhere you go around here is just cement, and brick, and there's none of that flavor. Like, for example, in China, you can go down the back streets and you can feel it, you know? I see a very little bit of that here in Cheonan City. On Arirang news, every time they give cultural events for the weekend it's all in Seoul. All the culture is in Seoul! There is nothing here, it's the wasteland. I know Jay likes to say to us, "Oh, you know what Cheonan means? Best paradise under heaven!" I said, well then they better redefine that term paradise because it ain't here man! This ain't it! So, that's what he told me, he's so proud of it. Yeah, I just don't see a lot of culture here. That's just my opinion.

Tell me about the Korean people that you've met here.

Um. The people I've met here are just like people all over the world. There are good ones and there are bad ones. Most of the people whom I've met have been very nice. My laundry lady, Mrs. Sung, she's extremely nice. The pizza people are very sweet and nice. My Korean family that kind of adopted me during my stay here—very nice. So, yeah, would I say that Korean people are so warm and gracious like the books say? Ehhh, I don't know. I don't think so. I think a lot of them are a little afraid of us. I talked to this one girl whom I wanted to ask out on a date, and she said, "Oh no! My mother would never let me go out with an American!" I said, "Why?" And she said, "Well, because my parents feel that Americans come from a very violent culture, and all you guys want to do over here is rape, kill, and steal." And I said, "Oooh, well, then I guess the wedding is off too then!" So, I said, "Well, there is nothing I can do if you think that's our culture, and that our culture is violent, but I'm not like that." So, I don't know. I guess, generally, the Korean people have been pretty nice to me. I don't know if it's a phony niceness, like maybe they say, "*Oooh, there's a chance to be nice to an American or a foreigner!*" You know? But generally they've been pretty cool. I haven't really had any bad experiences—EXCEPT, that the Korean drivers suck! I almost got killed about twenty times here! People drive on the fricking sidewalk! But anyways, Korean people are nice. Are they overly nice? No. And from my experience, not as friendly as Chinese people. The Korean people at work are kind of stand-offish. Like the other night I stayed late at the school, and before I went home I saw that they were all eating. I wasn't invited. Nobody asked me, "Would you like to sit down and eat with us? Would you like a little something to take home?" No. They were all just feeding their faces. Anyways, I felt like I was on the outside at that moment. But on the other hand, I met this Korean family at Songyung University while I was playing basketball. A mother, father, and two little girls. They invited me over for Christmas. They want to take me out next Tuesday for a good-bye party. They gave me a Valentine's day candybar. I mean, you know? I checked my email the other day, and there was a congratulations e-card in there that said "You made it!" So, they've got hearts of gold. And there is good and bad in every culture. Fortunately, I think, most of the people I've known have been very nice. I run into people who will wave to me from their cars and stuff like that too.

I remember you were saying how you thought customer service in Korea has been great.

Oh yeah! Customer service is great! I bought this lamp for sixty-thousand won. It stopped about a month and a half after I bought it, and I thought *Oh fudge!* Anyways, I took it back to the place and I said, "Here is my receipt. My lamp doesn't work. I don't know if it's the light bulb or what." Well, they took it, pulled the switch out, and fixed it up, and bang, ready to go. So I said, "How much?" They said, "Oh no, no, no, service, service." I said, "Cool!" And when I go get a pizza, I always get a pint of coke, extra pickles, and all this extra stuff—for free. I always refuse the coke because I don't like to drink that, but they always want to throw in all of this free stuff, and I keep thinking, how do they make any money, you know? Another thing, I went to a PC room a few weeks ago (internet café) and I paid for three hours. So the guy comes up and asks me if I want coffee. Then he comes up to me with a little cup of hot chocolate. So, I told him "No thank you, I don't want anything." So he comes back and says, "Five hours." I said, "What five hours? I only signed up for three?" And he says "Oh, two hours service." So, unfortunately, I couldn't stay for the extra two hours, but I've gotten extra hours like that before. So, yeah, customer service here is very cool. Another thing I like about Korea, which I wish Mr. Bush would listen to, is the passenger trains. I mean, Bush has hacked away at Amtrak, trying to get rid of all the funding. Passenger trains in Korea are wonderful. I've only taken them two or three times now, but they're great. I like them very much. So, passenger trains and customer service are very high here. I give them big marks for that.

What differences do you see between Koreans and foreigners here in Korea?

Oh, Koreans are much nicer than foreigners. Foreigners here are pricks. Oh God! They're awful. I've run into so many downtown, I've said "hi" to them, and they just stare at me. And I know, by God, that they can speak English. I can tell if someone is Russian. I don't know how I can tell, but they just have this look on their face—they're just Russian. But I've run into Americans, Australians, and others, and I think they got this 'thing' like they want to be the only foreigner in Korea. They probably say, "I want everybody to look at me, and to fuss over me, and to be impressed by me!" And then it's, "Oh shit! Here comes another one! God, I feel threatened!" You know? "Oooh, now there's two of us! That might take some of the attention away from me!" And I have said "hi" to just about everyone I have met. I would say that's close to about a hundred people. I have gotten maybe about ten responses. So, yeah, foreigners are pricks here. Korean people, even though they'll stare at you and giggle and laugh or whatever, most of them will at least say "hi" to you. Most of them will. But yeah, I think it's that some people want to be the only foreigner in Korea, but ehhh, sorry! That ship sailed long ago! So, I just don't talk to foreigners anymore. I did run into some very nice people from

India, they were very friendly. I also ran into some African people, I don't know what country they were from. But one girl was studying Korean. She was very nice. But I'm talking about foreigners overall, they can be very stuck-up. I got so mad at this one foreign woman who was walking under this tunnel on her way downtown, and I said "hi, good morning" to her. She just looked at me. I kept thinking, "Bitch? Don't you know how to say 'hello' to someone?" Oh, I lost it. I was really angry that day. All she had to do was say "hello." That's all she had to do. I wasn't asking her for a date, I sure as hell didn't want to sleep with her; I just wanted her to say "hello." Westerners don't hang together here. They don't even seem to want to talk to each other. So, yeah, there's something wrong here. Overall, Koreans are friendlier than foreigners, by far. This is in my experience. Maybe that's not true for anyone else, but, it's true for me.

*Do you feel that there is ever a culture clash between Koreans and foreigners, or the Korean and foreign staff at the school that you work in? If so, why and in what way?

Yes. I would say that there is a culture clash. Just the way they run the place. There is no communication. The boss assumes that we're (the foreign staff) gonna know. Or, maybe that's just the way Korean people work. The boss knows, but we don't have to know, but we'll know at the last minute so we'll eventually get it done. Jay doesn't tell us jack. He doesn't tell us anything. We're supposed to juggle everything at the last second. And even Jay himself said, "Well, I know there is a communication problem between us." I remember, I think I got on Jay's wrong side in the beginning, because for me, the ol' buzzer goes off at six o'clock p.m. At six p.m., I'm going home. I'm not hanging around work to suck up with the boss, or be kissy-face with the employees. I'm just thinking, *Get the hell away from me, I've been here all day, I want to go home, and I got a forty minute walk ahead of me.* Jay seemed to be put-off by it at first. So I said, "Jay, that's not the way I work. I can get work done sitting at home, listening to the radio or the TV, but I can't do it here sitting in the classroom cuddling up with you or God knows who else stays here." I've got too much to do and I can't concentrate at work after-hours. It must be a work-ethic clash or something, you know? In Korea, it's all about family, and work is their life. For me, it's not my life. Korean people are like married to their work. I'm not. It's like, *Okay, the bell goes off and I'm out of here!* I mean, Sam and the rest of them would 'cuddle up' together at the office, I would have my jacket and shoes on and say, "Okay, see you guys tomorrow." One night, Jay asked me, "Where are you going?" I said, "I'm going home! I gotta get outta here! I'm stressed! I gotta go home and do a ton of stuff (prepare for tomorrow's lesson)!" So he says, "Well, can't you do it here?" I said, "No! I can't do it here! Because I'm at work! I want to go home. I can focus better there." Then, after about two or three conversations about this, he finally got it. He finally understood the way I do things. After that, he left me alone. He didn't bother me anymore. I guess, my work was good, and he saw the way I did my job and started to respect it. He saw me come in over an hour early every morning to work. I never came in fifteen minutes before the morning bell rung. I would prepare and get my classes ready at quarter to nine every morning. I would be in early, photocopying, getting my room ready, and cleaning my room. And once Jay started to watch how I do things and the results I was getting from teaching his precious little money makers (students), he left me alone. And then he started saying, "Oh, have a good night! See you in the morning!" So, yeah, it was the work thing and the overall communication was bad. He doesn't tell us shit, and we're supposed to figure it out. Like we're supposed to read his mind. I don't know if that goes on in every Korean company—God, I hope not! But if it does, that's not gonna work for me.

***Tell me about the garden party.*

Oh God, yes! The lovely Garden party! There was this Garden Party Jay was having at the school so that he could impress all the parents and all the little kids; have them run around and have a bonfire and barbecue and so forth. Well, I'm not the most sociable person in the world. I try to be nice to people, and I can talk to them on the street and stuff, but I hate these phony, kissy-face, bullshit parties. I'm not a party person. I went to my sister's wedding in nineteen-seventy-six for twenty minutes and couldn't stand the shit at the reception and left. I don't like big gatherings and large groups. I'm kind of a lone wolf. Anyways, Chris, Jay's assistant, said to me, "Uh, Rob, uh, we're having a garden party this Friday." I told him, "I'm not coming. I'm not gonna be there. I hate parties." He said, "Oh, okay." And that was the end of it. This is on a Monday. So Friday, it was an hour before going home and Jay said, "Oh, Rob, you're not coming to the party?" I said, "I'm going home." He said, "Oh no, garden party." I said, "Oh no. I'm going home. I don't have to go." He said, "Who said you don't have to go?" I said, "Chris. Chris said it was okay." "Oh but you gotta go," he says to me. I said, "No, I don't have to go. I can't stand parties. I get a knot in my stomach and I can't sit there and deal with all of that shit. I've been with these kids all day, I'm going home." So, Jay said, "Well, just try, just try." So I said, "Okay Jay, I'll try. I'll see if I can go." When it was getting closer to the witching hour of six o'clock, my stomach started getting more and more knotted and I kept thinking, *Oh God, now I gotta run around with all these little buggers all night long*. I'll have to say, "Oh yes, yes, your little son is sooo cute," and all that bullshit. Anyways, so, five minutes to six I said to Jay, "Jay, sorry, I can't stay. I gotta go home. I can't do this." Just as I walked out the door he says, "But you promised!" And I said, "I didn't promise anything! I said that I would try. And I can't!" So he started yelling, "You know, this is really important to me! This is for our school. We really need you to stay!" So I said, "Okay. I'll try." So I went back in. But I couldn't do it. I said, "No, Jay, I can't do it." And Jay was already in his truck digging something out. I said to Julie (Korean teacher), "I'm outta here. I'm going home. I ain't doing this." I get out to the road and just turn the corner, and Jay starts yelling at me, "Where are you going! You just can't leave! I'm the boss! I'm the boss! Get back here! We're gonna have a talk!" I said, "Oh God! Yes we are! We're gonna have a talk all right." So I stormed back in. I said, "Fine! I'll stay at your God-almighty party!" So I took my stuff, I walked back into the school, I slammed my shoes into the little cabinet, and I slammed the door. He said, "Rob! Get out here!" I said, "Now what do you want? I'm going to your party!" "Get back here! We gotta have a talk in the back right now." So I said, "Fine, Jay, let's talk." So I went back there and he pulled that, "You said you were gonna stay." I said, "Jay, I said I was gonna try." He yelled, "You know, I'm very upset!" I told him, "Do you see the tears in my eyes, Jay? Do you think I'm in a great mood right now? The thought of hanging around these people tonight made me a nervous wreck. I don't want to be around here. Why can't you just respect that?" I told Jay that Chris gave me the understanding that I didn't have to go. I asked him why he had to wait until Friday at five o'clock to tell me that I had to go. You know? So I asked him why we couldn't talk about this earlier in the week. He knew how I felt about this. So he said, "Oh, I'm sorry. I guess there was a communication problem." I said, "Oh yes there was." So I told him, "I'll tell you what, I'll make a deal with you. If you let me go home and don't hassle me anymore about this party, because my stomach is a mess right now and I feel like I'm sick, I will write a letter to all the parents and explain why I wasn't there." So, Jay agreed with that. I told him that I would do that. So, after we parted ways, things got back to good terms after that. I told him that I wasn't there to screw him over; it's just that I didn't want to be in a situation like that. So, I guess, during the party people were asking where I was and he made an announcement that I couldn't handle it. And I have even turned down invitations to people's houses for dinner. I just told them that I didn't want to go. I just don't want to go into that uncomfortable environment, you know? I'm sure the parents would ask, "Oh, how's my son doing?" Ugh, while he's running around grabbing at your ears and stuff. It's like, ugh, I don't want to deal with that. And most of the parents can hardly speak English, and I just didn't have the energy level or the interest level at that point to go and deal with that. So, I wrote the parents a letter and I explained everything. I said that I didn't even go to my own graduation party. I skipped the whole thing. I said that I'm not a party person, so please respect that. I said, "Thank you." Of course I could throw up now for saying it, but I made the statement in the letter that Jay is a wonderful boss to work for. Oh God! I wish I could have that letter back! Anyways, he seemed okay at that time, at least, he wasn't as bad then as he is now. Of course after reading my letter, all the parents were cool about it. Everyone was very nice about it and they understood. I even told them, "I'm sorry, but I can't accept invitations to your homes for dinner, I'm just not that kind of person." I also told them that if they ever need to talk, here I am. And, if you want to talk about it some more—why I don't go to parties—I'm free. Come in and talk to me anytime. And they were totally cool about it. They were fine. And again, the boss made a big, hysterical deal about it, but oh well, that's life.

Why do you think there is such a communication problem? Why was it such a difficult thing for him to grasp the idea that this is not your thing?

Oh, because Jay is the boss. He likes to be recognized. He likes to be right. He thinks, *It's my way or the highway*. He got his little business degree and he's all proud of that, and mommy and daddy work at the school so he can impress them by throwing his weight around and showing them what a smooth and cool operator he is. He put his money in and got himself a school, so automatically he becomes principal, even though he has no education or background whatsoever. He has no clue what he's doing. I even asked him one time, "What's your background?" He said, "Uhhh, business degree." I said, "And?" That was it! Total silence. And I thought, *Oh my God, dear God, now I know what we're in for*. Because if you ever try to apply for a principal position, they ask you how many years you've been teaching, your administrative background, have you ever been in disciplinary roles or anything. There's a list a mile long. This guy just buys a fricking school like a McDonald's and he becomes principal? I mean, what the hell is that? So, yeah, you know? I'm sorry I forgot your question. What was it again?

Why do you think there is such a communication problem?

Yeah, that's it. It's because he wants to be the boss. He even wanted me to make sure that his name was mentioned by the kids in their graduation speech. He said, "Don't forget to mention 'Jay', kids!"

So that was his idea?

Yeah, yeah. And I said, "Well, kids, I guess he is the boss and he is the principal," but I didn't exactly push it on them. I said to the kids, "Let's mention Mrs. Jung (the cook) because she doesn't get a lot of credit and she works very hard in the kitchen." But yeah, he came right into my classroom and sat his ass down and said, "Oh, don't forget to mention Jay!" He said that with this sour pickle smile on his face. I could have just strangled him, awww

Christ. Where is Jeffrey Dahmer when we need him? But anyways. It's a power trip thing for him, and he loves it. I've seen him at the end of the day talking to the kids and he tells them to say "thank you" to the teachers. And then he'll specifically say, "And say, *thank you Jay*." And I'm thinking, *this is sick!* This guy is fricking twisted! He has to have his name mentioned everywhere! And it's a power trip with him. He's mister big shot. By-God, he had to get a school and be the principal. That's why there's a communication problem because he thinks he's Mister Big Shot and we're just nobodies. What he says, goes, and don't argue. He thinks, *If I don't tell you about it, oh well, you'll learn to do it, foreigner*. Absolutely.

*But there is also the other foreign staff, like the Korean teachers. Do you feel that there are ever any communication problems between the foreign teachers and the Korean teachers?

Oh, all the time. They do nothing anyways. They sit at that front desk, doing their nails, looking in the mirror, playing on the website. They don't do crap for me anyways, so I just blow them off. I just think of the female Korean teachers as people who are just taking up space and making money that I could have for myself. Even though I didn't like the last Korean teachers' personalities (the ones that quit), they did their jobs and they did it well. If I needed a sign made for something, it was done, right away. I asked one of our present Korean teachers in the middle of February if she could do me a favor and get me a sign that says 'February' on it. It was February third already and I needed it done ASAP. So, she said, "Oh yeah, sure." Well, that was February third, and February kept coming along. So, I asked the boss, "Oh boss? Do you think you could get a February sign for my room, for the kids?" He said, "Oh yeah, yeah, I'll take care of it for ya." Yeah, February twenty-second comes around and I'm sitting in the classroom making my own February sign. Those teachers are useless, dammit! Useless. Communication problem? Yeah. All I have to do is say "hi" to them (female Korean teachers) and they just squeak and laugh and run to the other side, and I just say, "Whatever." So, I do it myself. If I need something done, I just do it myself. So yes, there is a communication problem. I try to talk to them but they don't know what the hell you're saying.

*How do you think the Korean staff feels about us?

Oh, I think they like us less now that you and Jane showed up.

*Really?

Oh, God, yes. Because Sam and I, even though Sam sucks up to them, I just kind of went my own way and did my job the best I could. You and Jane say a lot of stuff that pisses them off. The most I would do is sigh and say, "Oh, God, okay, I'll do it." So then I go back to my classroom until he would run in there later and ask something else. But, I knew I was only staying here for a year, and unfortunately I put up with too much shit, and maybe I shouldn't have. That's why I said that you and Jane were a breath of fresh air when you came plowing through the doors. Every time you go after him (the boss) I think, *God bless you Melissa!* You and Jane, God bless you a thousand times over! Maybe I don't have the balls to go after him, or maybe not the interest. I knew I was here for a year. I started counting down three-hundred and sixty-five days starting on the second day. So, I knew I was eventually leaving. And this guy (the boss) is so whacked out anyways; he doesn't know what he's doing, so to ask him anything is pointless anyways. I think the foreign staff likes us less now. And me, I'm old news now because I'm on my way out. And you see it. When the new teachers come, they all come running up to them with open arms. And then three months into it they go, "Yeah, yeah, sure, I'll make the February sign! As soon as I check my face in the mirror!"

Do you think that the Korean staff thinks that the foreign staff is strange or lazy in anyway?

I don't know what they think. I honest to God can't figure out what they're thinking. But, if they would ever comment to me that I'm lazy, I would just reply, "Yeah, right. Like I'm the one sitting in front of the computer all day doing my fingernails." I'm busting my ass nine hours a day. I don't care what they think about us. And I really don't know, because they put on their little smiley faces.

What were some of your best moments?

Best moments in Korea? Ummm… let's see. When my kids hit it perfectly on Halloween. When my kids hit it perfectly on Christmas. When my kids hit it perfectly the other day at graduation. Those were my best moments. Why? Because it showed everybody that I did my job the best I could. I put a lot of effort into them. I heard the applause from the parents. We worked very hard on our Halloween song and we worked very hard on our Christmas play, as yours did too. We also worked very hard preparing for the graduation ceremony—and Thanksgiving. And by 'hit it' I mean that they pulled it off great. It was show time and they did it almost perfectly. I saw the gratitude in the parents' faces and I heard the applause, and I felt good. I was proud of everybody in my class and I said, "By God, we did it. We did it again, alright." You know? Those were very good moments. Also, playing basketball during the summer was a great moment too. It sounds boring, but I lost fifteen to twenty pounds doing it. It was wonderful. Also, the people I met gave me some good moments too. There haven't been a whole lot of best moments in Korea because I haven't really experienced Korea like others have. I'm not really a restaurant person, and I haven't traveled much because I just wanted to make money and go home. Next time if I come back I'll travel a lot more so I'll have more 'best moments'. Tomorrow, at six o'clock is going to be a 'best moment'. Absolutely. Last day tomorrow. Six o'clock, once elementary gets done, it's adios folks! But seeing the results of my work and all the effort I put into it, that makes me feel good. I hear the parents say that I did a good job and that I was a good teacher. That gave me a good feeling.

What were some of your worst moments?

Three-hundred and sixty-five days of Kid's College, well, until you girls walked in the door and brought some laughter and enjoyment. I hated my confrontations with Sam (another English teacher). We had a lot of tensions between us. Also, being almost hit four or five times by Korean drivers, that sucked. Eating kimchi… that definitely wasn't a highlight of my life here in Korea. Sorry, I just don't like kimchi and Korean food. Too hot and spicy. Worst moments? Oh. All the days the boss would pull shit on me at the last minute and add stress to my life. That kind of stuff, you know? The first time I realized summer wasn't going to end for a long time. Ugh. Korean summers are bad. I happened to get here just in time to experience the hottest summer in ten years, and boy did we get it. Oh my God! The middle of May to October. October fourteenth was the first time I saw my breath in the air when I walked to school in the morning. So yeah, the heat was a four-month worst moment. Ugh, it was nasty. Anymore worst moments? Umm, no. Well, the fire in our apartment, but you guys were here to ease the funk. I got through it okay because I knew I was going home soon. I really didn't give a shit. Whereas you guys were in a much tougher position because you guys had six more months to go, or whatever. Me, I only had a few weeks left once the fire hit, so I could stick it out. But yeah, that was a worst moment. Also at that time, as the fire was being put out, Jane and I called the boss and asked him to come and help us, and he answered the phone drunk off his ass and said that he couldn't come because he was at a party. That was a very cold, nasty moment for me. That was colder than any winter wind I've felt here. I told my professor friend in San Fran, that there was nothing my boss could do—nothing he could give me or say to me—to repair that damaged relationship. Boy, that was it! That was the last draw. When he pulled that 'I can't help you guys now' shit, that really proved that he didn't care about us.

Do you fee that, overall, you've been treated fairly here in Korea?

Oh yeah. By the boss, no. By Korean people, yes. My laundry lady has been extremely fair. She has charged me so little for cleaning my clothes. I would feel so bad about it that I would give her an extra one thousand won and say "just take it, it's okay." She works such long hours. I've gone to places where they wanted to give me free candy because I was friendly to them. Yeah, I would say that I've been treated fair here. I've had no racial problems here. Everybody is overall nice to me. One day I went to Burger King and ended up making friends with everybody there. They'd all say "Hi Bob!" from the kitchen area. The other day they gave me free French fries. So, you know, it's just about being nice to people. So, yeah, I've been treated fairly, but I think it's a two-way street. If you're nice to them, they'll be nice to you. Fairness here goes along with customer service here. It's very good.

If you had to do it all over again, what would you change?

Well, oh God, I hate that question because it's twenty-twenty hind sight. Okay, what would I do different? Let me put it this way, my advice to someone who's thinking about doing this. Part of the game is getting a university job. Here in Korea, they want you to have experience before you get your university job. So, if you are in any major metropolitan city in the United States (or any other English speaking country), try to find an English school there and teach for a year there if you can—even if it's volunteer. Then you can say, okay, I've taught for a year and now I have the experience. Try to avoid getting your experience at a hagwon in Korea. A lot of university teachers will tell you that they feel sorry for you if you work in a hagwon. So, avoid the hagwons if you can. Try to dance around that and get to a university if you can do it. Fulfill your experience in your own country first and then apply to a Korean university, especially if you live in a city. Get that year behind you so that you can be ready to teach at a university. Because what we did is our baptism by fire. You gotta do the hagwon first before you do anything else. This way you can be confident to say, *you know what, I have experience teaching kids so I don't need to apply to another hagwon.* But, what would I change? Nothing. Nothing. Even though I had to put up with a lot of shit, I learned a lot. It's been a learning experience. I know now, I wouldn't deal with it again. I will never do this again—never—no way! Now I can go home and tell people, "be careful!" If anyone says to me, "Oh, I've been thinking about doing that and it sounds like a lot of fun," I'll just say, "Oh yeah? Here's the address of Kid's College and you tell me after a year how much fun you had!" I mean, I'm not knocking the little kids because the ones I had were very smart, even though they generally drove me a little crazy sometimes. Overall, they were pretty good. So, I just focused on the kids and did the best I could. But I'm sure I have a few more gray hairs because of this place. Overall, I don't think I would change anything. It worked out generally okay. I saved the money I needed and I got the year experience behind me. I could say that I stuck it out and I made it. I did it. It's over. I think I'm a richer person because of this experience. I know I can now go home and say that I know more about Korea than I did before. I have more friends in Korea than I had before. You know? I'm glad I came and I'm glad I'm leaving. If I had to return, it's possible for me to live here the rest of my life. I told my mom, "It wasn't great, it wasn't horrible, it was okay." I told my mom that I had a place to sleep, a place to shit, and a place to shower. That's all I needed. Korea is not like Bangladesh or anything, you know. It's pretty modern, even though there are a few little inconveniences. But it's not life or death.

What are you going to miss about Korea?

You guys, of course. I'll miss my Korean family, my friend Sull-lee, my laundry lady, the guy at Burger King, the pizza lady, and the university basketball courts

After Rob swore in the conversation he had with me that he wasn't going to work in Korea ever again, I got in touch with him after about two years and found that he was on his way back there! He was in a financial situation once again, after he had spent all of his savings he accumulated in his last trip to Korea. He accepted a contract at a hagwon in the countryside near Cheonan city. I kept in touch with him for a few months into his contract, and sadly, as he was in Korea, his mother had died back in the United States. Unfortunately, he was unable to afford to fly back home for the funeral. So, he became depressed and politely asked that he lose contact with me for awhile. I have not heard from him since.

Reflections

As you can see through the conversations, experiences vary from positive to negative. Nate Chang's experience was certainly a positive one. I ran into him several times during his contract, and was always upbeat and excited to talk about it. Rob, on the other hand, had a much grimmer story. As I mentioned earlier, because he was a loner, Rob lacked a proper support and social system. He couldn't get accustomed to the food and the Korean-style of communication. With Rob, there were many things I agreed with and there were some things I strongly disagreed with. I agreed with the little things such as the good customer service and kind disposition of the Korean people. I also agreed with the lack of organization and communication between the Korean and Western staff. The things I strongly disagreed with are worth mentioning. First, I don't believe that one of the two types of people that come to Korea is losers. Anyone who goes to a foreign country to live and work has somewhat of an adventurous personality, and is independent-minded and success-driven—even Rob. People who come to Korea to teach are definitely not losers. Second, I strongly disagree that Westerners do not take the time to talk to each other or get to know one another. I believe that most Westerners that are seen in Korea are fairly new to the country, and they are experiencing some kind of isolation or loneliness. They look to other Westerners frequently for support and companionship. This is apparent in clubs, bars, and cafes, especially places that Westerners or foreigners gather in. Rob was unfamiliar with this because, as a loner, he never took the opportunity to visit a Western/foreigner bar or café. He stayed in his apartment where he felt safe and 'productive'. Third, there is nothing about Korea that is a 'wasteland' as Rob expressed. Cities do tend to be concrete, busy, and full of architecture; however, there are back streets and countryside neighborhoods where 'culture' can certainly be felt. There are palaces that have been preserved for thousands of years. There are street festivals and fairs, and traditional performances at many community centers in big cities and small towns. Again, all this was missed by Rob because he chose not to leave his safe haven. He walked to and from school everyday, with an occasional stop at the pizza shop. That is hardly enough roaming to see any actual 'culture'.

Overall, I hope all of the conversations were candid enough for you to get a good idea about how Korea has been experienced by individuals with varying opinions. I hope this can be valuable to you when you make specific decisions regarding your potential teaching job.

Chapter 9:
Important Information to Refer to Once You Arrive in Korea

When traveling to any country, it is always important to know a little bit about that country, especially if you're planning on living and working there. The following is some crucial information that can help you while living in South Korea. The phone numbers, especially, have helped me during my two years in the country.

Basic information:
Current president: Lee Myung Bak

Currency: Korean Won. Check www.xe.com for the current exchange rate between won to dollar.

Language: Korean. Dialects differ depending on what province you visit.

Capital City: Seoul, population: approximately 10,356,000 (http://ipedia.net/information/Seoul).

Population of South Korea: approximately 48,379,392 as of 2008 (https://www.cia.gov/library/publications/the-world-factbook).

Emergency number: 119

Emergency number for criminal activity: 112

Crime: Extremely low. According to recent statistics on the website Nationmaster.com (http://www.nationmaster.com), assaults, burglaries, and murders in South Korea were very low compared to the United States. Last year, assaults in Korea totaled 14,925, while in the U.S.A. there were 2,238,480. There were also 3,027 burglaries in Korea compared to 2,151,875 in the U.S.A. Murders totaled 955 in Korea, while murders totaled 16,204 in the U.S.A.!

Important websites:
The immigration bureau is where you can find information on immigration-related issues. The website is:
http://www.immigration.go.kr/indeximmeng.html.

Other helpful sites are:
http://www.korea.net/
http://english.seoul.go.kr/ (Hi Seoul website)
http://www.customs.go.kr (Korea Customs Services Website)
www.daveseslcafe.com (You can find ESL jobs here and participate in conversation boards with other expatriates).
http://global.seoul.go.kr/ (This is an extremely helpful website that has information that is valuable for every expatriate in Korea).

The Seoul Global Center offers consultation services for foreigners living and working in Korea. It is staffed by many volunteers that speak different languages (mostly English). The center provides information on special events for foreign communities, immigration and visa issues, labor issues, driving issues, training, and help for foreign migrants and marriage immigrants. I have used the Seoul Global center to help me with questions regarding labor law and taxes, as well as how and where to get my driver's license. The staff there is very helpful and courteous, and if they don't know the answer to your question, they will find out for you. It is that simple, and I recommend you use it frequently. It will give you piece of mind knowing that information is right at your fingertips—in English!

Getting your Korean driver's license:
You may want to get a driver's license while you're in Korea. This can be a very simple process. There are many driver's license facilities in Korea. The one I used was in Seoul, near the World Cup Stadium in Mapo-Gu (West of downtown Seoul). They were very helpful and courteous there, and the staff spoke English very well. You will need to bring your passport, your Alien I.D. card, three passport-sized photos, cash (approximately twenty-thousand won), and your original driver's license form your home country. You must go to the facility during operating hours, present your driver's license from

your home country, and fill out an application. Once you have done this, you will have to take a test. The test has twenty questions and the English is not so good. Actually, the questions are quite grammatically incorrect! However, you'll get the point of what they're trying to ask you. It's a computer test and you can touch the screen to select the correct answers. Once you have done this and receive your test score (the testing time is less than an hour), you must get a vision test. The test typically takes about fifteen seconds and it is administered in the same building as your computer test. Once you are done with each step of the testing, the staff will escort you in the right direction. You will then go to the main counter downstairs for processing. After about thirty minutes (and that's on a busy day!) your new license will be presented to you. Keep in mind that you will have to surrender your original driver's license in order to get your Korean one. If you are going back to your home country on vacation at any time, you can return to the Driver's license facility and exchange your Korean license for your original one. However, you will have to show them your plane ticket. Once you return to Korea, you can exchange it back. You will not have to take the test and the eye exam a second time. When I left Korea for good, the driver's license facility allowed me to keep both my Korean license and original license. I was also told by the clerk that it is possible to receive an international license at the same time you receive your Korean license, but you must present an airline reservation receipt or a ticket to prove that you are travelling outside of Korea and that you are in need of an international license. The cost for an international license will be extra and you will need to have an additional passport-sized photo. The Korean license can actually be used in certain English-speaking countries. It is best to check with your home country's Department of Motor Vehicles if you can use your Korean license back home. At the time of this writing, a Korean driver's license cannot be used to drive in the United States.

Opening a bank account:
It is a good idea to open a Korean bank account so that you can get a debit card and have your pay directly deposited into it. There are numerous banks in South Korea. If you are planning on wire transferring your money to your home country, I recommend that you choose a bank that offers this service and has low fees and good exchange rates. Nonghyup bank offers free accounts and fairly low wire transfer fees. They will even give you discounts on exchange rates after you've done several exchanges and wire transfers with them. Other banks are Shinan Bank, Korea Exchange Bank (KEB), and Citibank. Since Citibank is global, you'll be able to keep your account and debit card once you leave Korea and use them in other countries as well.

To open up an account, all you need is your passport, foreign I.D., and some money to deposit. Check with the banks to see if there are minimum limits on initial deposits, and fees associated with dipping below a certain balance. If you have a spouse, family member, or a boy/girlfriend, don't even think about getting a joint account in a Korean bank—they don't exist! There is only one account holder per account, and if you want someone else to have access to it, you will just have to give that person your debit card and pin number. You can, however, list a beneficiary on your account to ensure that your loved one gets your money if something were to happen to you. There is no check-writing in Korea, only cash, debit and credit cards, and direct deposits.

Questioning Yourself: Is It the Right Decision?

Every once in a while I started to feel very sentimental about things during my stay in Korea. I sat and thought about all of my friends at home that I left behind. I started to get lonely just a little bit in my room, and I started to ask myself questions. Did I do the right thing by taking a job overseas and coming to Korea? Will everything at home fall apart while I'm gone? But then I would snap back into reality and remind myself that working and living in another country, even temporarily, could be a once in a lifetime thing. This was an opportunity that was wise of me to take advantage of at that particular point in my life. I wasn't married (although it's not uncommon for people working in Korea to bring their spouses along), I wasn't tied down to a job, and I knew what my financial situation would be like if I didn't go. At that time, it was the right thing to do. I had to remember that my family, my friends, and my home would still be there when I returned to my country, and I would have the rest of my life to spend with them. Even after all the griping and complaining that Rob did about his experience in Korea, he never regretted it. He acknowledged that it was the right decision to make at that point in his life, and it made him a better person overall.

If I were to give two of the most important pieces of advice to individuals planning on living and working in Korea, they would most certainly be the following:

- Remember to be extremely flexible
- Take every single thing with stride

You will constantly encounter miscommunications, changes in your schedule, errors, misjudgments, and a bit of awkwardness. You have to remember, the foreign teacher is really considered as a 'product' in Korea. The school with the best product gets the most business. This can be a bit jarring and insulting once in awhile, making one feel like a spectacle in a zoo. But you have to remember to *'play it'*. Like some of my students in a company English class once told me, "Melissa, assume that you are the movie star, and play it up. If people stare and make comments, smile for the camera. Soak up the recognition and turn it into something glamorous." These students had the right idea. In all honesty, even though you are the 'product', you are simultaneously a 'celebrity'. Just like real celebrities are products. In the town that I live in, I am one of, perhaps, four foreigners. Of course, people stare at me and children sometimes point, especially if I'm walking my two big dogs. I have to just remember that they are looking at me in curiosity and wonder.

On a final note, it is important to remember that the way you do things is not necessarily the right way. When beginning your new working venture in South Korea, always keep in mind that there are a new set of customs and rules you must get used to in order to make your venture successful. Being courteous goes a long way. Author Kurt F. Weigelt wisely mentions this in his 1993 book, **Culture Bridge**.

> *"Politeness means conforming to the customs of etiquette and proper behavior. Because the customs of etiquette and proper behavior differ from one country to another, we cannot say that one nation's people are more polite, or less polite, than another's. Rudeness is when a person knowingly violates those customs. If the person unknowingly violates those customs, then he is not rude, just ignorant of custom."*

In my opinion, you can only claim ignorance for so long before the local people in your host country begin despising you. Take the time to learn the etiquette and customs of the Korean people, and always be conscious of your behavior. Your adaptation and acceptance will go a long way, and doors will begin to open for future opportunities.

After spending some time proving myself to the local people of my town that I was a courteous, capable, and understanding person, opportunities began to fall into my lap.

I met many people who helped me when I needed help and who offered me jobs, as well as provided me services when I needed them. Learn from your environment, and even though you come as a teacher, let the people around you teach *you* as well. As long as you leave yourself open to every person, place, and experience around you, your journey will be a very rewarding one.

Good luck on your adventures in the Land of Kimchi, and—happy teaching!

Bibliography

Internet/Websites:

Central Intelligence Agency: The World Factbook website. "East and Southeast Asia; Korea, South." July 30, 2009. <https://www.cia.gov/library/ publications/the-world-factbook/geos/ks.html>

Dave's ESL Café website. "Jobs: Korean Job Board." Sperling, Dave. 2009. <http://www.daveseslcafe.com>
(You can find ESL jobs here and participate in conversation boards with other expatriates).

Economy Watch website. "South Korea Economy." 2004.
<http://www.economywatch.com/world_economy/south-korea/>

HiKorea website. "Visa." HiKorea, E-Government for Foreigners.
<http://www.hikorea.go.kr/pt/index.html>

Hi Seoul website. "Live in Seoul." 2009.
<http://english.seoul.go.kr/lh/work/employment.php>

Korean Consulate General in Los Angeles website. "Visa Information." 2009.
<http://www.koreanconsulatela.org/english/sub_index02.htm?pg=0201>

Korea Customs Service website. General information. 2009.
<http://www.customs.go.kr/>

Korea Focus website; Essays. "Causes for Corruption and Irregularities." Kim Myoung Soo. January – February 2000.
http://www.koreafocus.or.kr/design2/index.asp

Korea Herald Newspaper Online. "Expat Soapbox." Andrew. 2003.
<http://www.koreaherald.co.kr/>

Korea Herald Newspaper Online. "Expat Soapbox." Cindy. 2003.
<http://www.koreaherald.co.kr/>

Korea Herald Newspaper Online. "Expat Soapbox." FixerH. 2003.
<http://www.koreaherald.co.kr/>

Korea Herald Newspaper Online. "Expat Soapbox." Roy. 2003.
<http://www.koreaherald.co.kr/>

Korea Immigration Service website. "Visas and Immigration." (tables 1 and 2). 2009. <http://www.immigration.go.kr/indeximmeng.html>

Korea.net; Gateway to Korea website. "Social Welfare." 2009.
<http://www.korea.net/korea/kor_loca.asp?code=S01>

Nationmaster Statistic Encyclopedia website. "Korea, South." 2009.
<http://www.nationmaster.com/country/ks-korea-south>

Seoul Global Center website. "Living in Seoul; Accommodation; Residential Facilities." 2009.
<http://global.seoul.go.kr/global/view/working/working.jsp>

Wikipedia website. "History of South Korea." Last modified August 18, 2009.
<http://en.wikipedia.org/wiki/History_of_South_Korea>

Wikia Travel website. "Facts About the ESL Industry in Korea." 2005.
<http://korea.wikia.com/wiki/Facts_about_the_ESL_industry_in_Korea>

Wikia Travel website. "Welcome to the Korea Wiki." Date unknown.
<http://korea.wikia.com/wiki/Main_Page>

Books:

Weigelt, Kurt F. <u>Culture Bridge</u>. Si-sa-yong-o-sa, Inc. 1993.